Words of Faith

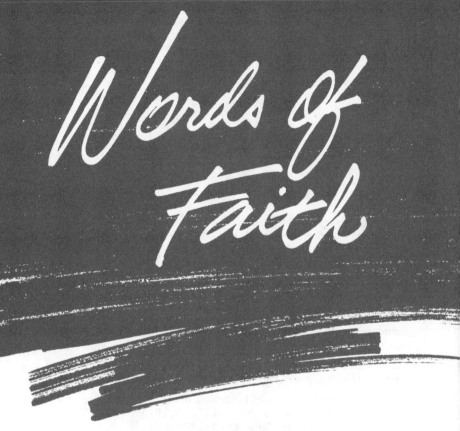

Words of Faith

A Devotional Dictionary

Charles S. Mueller

Publishing House
St. Louis

Copyright © 1985 by Concordia Publishing House
3558 South Jefferson Avenue, St. Louis, MO 63118-3968
Manufactured in the United States of America.

Library of Congress Cataloging in Publication Data

Mueller, Charles S.
    Words of faith.

    1. Theology—Dictionaries.   I. Title.
BR95.M84   1985   230'.41'0321   84-23874

---

1 2 3 4 5 6 7 8 9 10 MAL 94 93 92 91 90 89 88 87 86 85

Offered with love to Emily and Allison Mueller,
Stephen Filyo, and Rachel Stegemoeller,
our first four grandchildren
May this book be a blessing to them
and to all other grandchildren in God's world

Preface

Words. Beautiful words.

Among life's first tasks is that of mastering the meaning of words. Early meanings are so simple and direct. Who can misunderstand *mama, daddy, mine, love, no?* In our early years each word is tasted, flavored, and repeated again and again until if finally bubbles easily from our lips.

Isn't it odd that we are so careful to teach the fullest meaning of each new word the smaller child learns, but with the passing of the years do little more than correct pronunciations of those who are older? Are we assuming that if they can say the word correctly they understand it? Maybe that's why word tags develop mistaken meanings; why words are neutered; why communication gets difficult. We didn't know what the words mean.

That's not the way God meant it to be. God meant us to understand His words. He so means us to understand His words that He gave them to us in two forms. The first and best form is the living Word, Jesus Christ. The second is the words He inspired in Scripture through the apostles, prophets, and evangelists.

This book is written to bless those who care about His words, no matter what their form. It's for those who realize that if we misunderstand His words, God's intent for us gets confused. This book is written to define God's words. We want to grasp the key words of our faith, walking as close to their original meaning as possible. If we can know what the words meant as they were first chosen, we have a better chance of understanding the message God is sending us through them.

The encouragement for this book came from discussions with the faculty of Trinity Lutheran School, Roselle, IL. This group of superb teachers recognized the difficulty of communication. They suggested some kind of devotional dictionary that would explain the words we use in telling about our faith and its practice. They urged that the book be devotional, educational, and inspirational—for the young in faith. You can determine how well the following pages fit this standard.

One of my expectations in preparing this book is that it will be used by two or more Christians at a time. It's meant for discussion. In a class? Great! Parents and children together could be a great learning team, too.

I've also tried to practice repetition by weaving and reweaving key words through subsequent devotional studies in the book. Is there any educational maxim more fundamental than that repetition is the mother of study?

It is important that the readers take the Book in hand. For that reason each devotion has its Biblical reference. Within many of the individual studies there are varieties of encouragements to search the Scripture further. My thought was to force the development of the skill of finding verses quickly. My hope is that an understanding of the Biblical message will always be a companion benefit. However, one thing is sure: if you can't find the Bible passage it's tough learning its meaning.

Bishop Hans Lilje insisted that a primary internal task of the church is that of making the individual Christian think. Through these devotions I want to participate in this thought-producing process. I specifically prepared studies that will encourage thinking.

Now, some thanks. Throughout my lifetime I have had some great teachers. My mother, Aurelia Mueller, encouraged all her children to study and use words properly. I have a debt beyond repayment to great Christian teachers of words and the Word like Dr. Walter Wente, Dr. Lorenz Wunderlich, Dr. Al Glock, Dr. Walter Roehrs, and the sainted Dr. Martin Franzmann. They loved language and shared their enthusiasm with me when I was little more than a boy.

In the preparation of the manuscript I need to publicly state my appreciation to Nelda Piper and Judy White for their continued support. They worked hard getting this manuscript into usable form.

It's time to get to the words. My deepest desire is that they will be half as valuable to you in studying as they have already been to me in preparing. That would be something! I offer this all to you with the prayer of St. Paul in Colossians 3:16–17. Why don't we begin our journey together by seeking out these words? Search your Scriptures.

A.

ABSOLVE/ABSOLUTION (ab-ZOLV)　　　　*1 John 1:5–9*

What a wonderful first word for any book: absolve. Say it! *Absolve*. That word doesn't actually appear in the Bible. But the meaning of absolve surely does. I'll tell you more about it. You'll like it.

Absolve means *to loosen something that's sticking to you and carry it away*. It's something like "to clean." The thing that is sticking, and is then absolved by loosening, is always something bad; something dirty. It could be a wrong. Or guilt about a wrong. Or an accusation that you are doing something wrong. When any of those bad things are carried away, you are absolved, and you have received absolution (ab-so-LOO-shun). Let me tell you a make-believe absolve story. You are at school. It's recess time. The teacher tells you to go outside, When you get outside, you realize it's colder than you thought. Your cap is back on your desk. What do you do? You go back in and get it.

Now, suppose, when the whole class comes back from recess, that Dorothy, who sits next to you, says, "Teacher! My dollar is missing. I left it right here on my desk before recess. Someone took it!"

Everyone looks at you. You didn't take it. But they don't know you didn't. You turn red. You get gulpy. You say, "I didn't take it." But you can tell from the look in Dorothy's eyes that she's not sure. Others clearly don't believe you.

Just then, Ted comes in, late as usual. He goes up to the teacher and says, "Mrs. Homp, when we were going out to recess, I found this dollar lying on the floor. Someone must have dropped it. Maybe it fell out of a desk."

Whew! Absolved! The sticky possibility of being wrong or wronged is loosened and removed. Everyone laughs. Now they *know* you didn't do it.

In many churches, the pastor absolves the congregation at Sunday worship. The wrongs he absolves are real. The people have sinned. Actually, the pastor doesn't do the absolving. He

9

announces what God has absolved. He tells the people that when they sin and ask God for forgiveness, God will absolve.

See if you can find words about absolving in your hymnbook or in a Sunday order of service. The special loosening words that carry away our sins and replace them with forgiveness are called the *Words of Absolution*. Find them. Read them out loud. Take them apart. Think about what they mean.

ACOLYTE (AK-ko-lite)   *1 Samuel 2:18–19*

You've seen them. Acolytes, I mean. You've seen them in church. Sometimes they light candles. Sometimes they help when a baby is being baptized. Sometimes they assist during Communion. They usually dress like a pastor, with either a white robe (called an alb) or a white blouse (called a surplice) over a black robe (called a cassock).

An acolyte can be a teenager or a grown-up, but usually they are younger boys and girls between the ages of 9 and 12. They are helpers in the worship service.

The word *acolyte* means "a follower." I suppose that's because they follow after the pastor, or follow after the other assisting ministers, helping in any way they can. I've seen acolytes that carry the Bible, hand out certificates at confirmation, or bring in a banner when there is a procession.

Acolytes are important. They make a worship service nicer and neater. While the acolytes are acolyting, they not only help the congregation, they do special service before God. As the Wise Men of long ago brought gifts to Jesus (what a thrill that must have been!), or as the little boy gave his bread and fish to the Lord for special use (remember him?), acolytes have the satisfaction of giving to the Lord by serving.

A lot of churches have special training for acolytes. They get lessons on how to walk slowly and with dignity. They are shown when, and how, to bow. They are told which candles to light, and in what order. They are taught to show respect and serve as an example before the church. What do you think about that? Would you like to have some special acolyte training? Ask your pastor. Talk with him about what an acolyte might do in your congregation. Be ready to make some suggestions. Be ready to volunteer if he asks for helpers.

ADOPT/ADOPTION (uh-DOPT)   *Galatians 4:1–7*

Some kids are cruel. They say things that don't need to be said in ways that hurt. My friend Susie found that out. She found out how hurtful some kids can be. It happened when Kurt told her that he didn't like her, and the reason he didn't like her was, "You're adopted."

When that happened, Susie talked to her mom and dad. They explained that Kurt was probably upset with her and looked around for the meanest thing he could say. Strange that he picked something that wasn't mean or bad at all! *Adopt* isn't a bad word. It is a beautiful word, especially when it is explained how adopt and adoption work.

Her parents told Susie how they had gotten married. But they had no children. They wanted a little girl. They tried every way in the world to get one. Finally, they applied for a girl to adopt. And then they waited. "What a day when we were told we could have you," said Susie's mom, "Your dad and I screamed. We went wild phoning everyone we knew! We were so excited about adopting a wonderful little girl like you!"

Kurt might have thought that adopting was bad. But Susie sure didn't. Not after her parents' explanation! She realized she had been wanted. She had been waited for. She had been joyfully received. Her mom and dad didn't have to take her. They begged for a chance to take her into their home and hearts. Kurt tried to be mean. He really wasn't. Kurt was being stupid. He didn't know what he was talking about.

One of the great teachings in the Bible is that all of us are like Susie. We were "adopted" by God. Sin and our refusal to obey the Lord pushed us outside the family of faith. We were alone. We had no place to go. We had no home. But God loved us and wanted us. Our Father adopted us. No matter what the cost, He was determined to make us His own. He picked us out. He made us His own. He even gave us His name so that we are now sons and daughters of the Lord.

One of the ways we know we are God's children is through a prayer that our brother Jesus taught: Take a moment and look for that prayer in Luke 11:2. There's a word in that verse that says our adoption is real and complete. See it? It says you can call God, our "F _ _ _ _ _ ." You can call Him that because we are His children. Adopted, but really His children.

ADVENT (ADD-vent)   *Romans 8:28–29*

A good book or a movie has a beginning, a middle (or maybe a bunch of middles) and an end.

The beginning gets you into the story. It tells you where the story is taking place and who is involved. It sets the stage. That's what a beginning is for. Then comes the middle, with all the excitement and the parts that make you bite your fingernails. The middle part is usually the longest.

Finally, there is the end, which, in most stories, sees everything worked out. Some of the best ones end, "and they lived happily ever after."

Our church life is like an annually repeated story. Each year we tell it over again. We tell one part of the story every Sunday. As you listen to the story being told each year, you remember other parts and other things that happened. You see how things worked out in the life of Christ, or in the life of the people of God, and even among those who walk the way of faith now. It all works out.

During the year, we hear about the middle of the story, and we're reminded of the end. But there is a beginning. There is a time when the story starts. That annual new beginning has a name. It is called Advent. Advent is the start of the church's year. It begins the fourth Sunday before Christmas.

Does it surprise you that the beginning of the church year isn't Jan. 1? It shouldn't. Our story's beginning is before Christmas. During Advent we think about the coming of Jesus. That's what Advent means. Advent means "coming."

When someone or something is coming, we can talk about its *advent*. There could be an advent of your grandma (that would mean she's coming to see you), or an advent of your birthday (that would mean it's nearly here), or an advent of the end of school (that would mean there aren't many days till vacation). In the church, the word *advent* refers to the preparation for the coming of Christ.

And guess what! We believe that He is coming again. We believe there will yet be another advent. He will be coming back. He will come back to take us home. Isn't that wonderful? That means there will be yet another *advent*. Hooray!

ADVOCATE (ADD-vo-kate)   *1 John 2:1*

Advocate. Now there's a hard word! I doubt whether you've heard of it before. Could you guess what it means? It's not easy. Give up? Let me tell you. I'll tell you what advocate is by telling you an advocate story.

One day Kim was late coming in from recess. Mrs. Meyer, the teacher, had told the whole class that, "From now on, if anyone comes in late from recess, they will have to sit out in the hall for five minutes." When Kim came in late, Mrs. Meyer put her in the hall. She wouldn't listen to Kim's attempt to explain. Rules are rules.

Back in the classroom, Kim had an advocate. It was Marcie. Marcie said, "Mrs. Meyer, Kim was late because one of the first graders had her foot caught in the swing. She was crying and couldn't get out. Kim helped her." Immediately, Mrs. Meyer brought Kim in from the hall. She apologized to Kim and thanked Marcie for being Kim's advocate. An advocate is *someone who talks on your behalf.*

Here's another story. Laurie wanted a cat. She really wanted a cat. Any cat. Her sister Fran knew how much Laurie wanted a cat. But Laurie was afraid to ask her parents for a cat. She was afraid her mom would get mad, or her dad would say no. A cat was important to her. So, when Laurie couldn't speak up, Fran did. Fran talked to their mom and dad. Fran pleaded. She promised she would do anything if Laurie could have a cat. Fran helped her mom understand how important the cat was to Laurie. Guess what? Laurie got one. Fran was her advocate. She talked up on Laurie's behalf.

Do you have an advocate? You have at least one. You have an Advocate in heaven. That advocate is Jesus. He speaks up for you before God. He asks forgiveness from the Father for you. Our advocate, Jesus, always gets His way on our behalf. He gets His way because God loves Him. He is the best advocate there has ever been. Whatever we need from the Father He gets for us. Isn't that great?

Now a question for you. Have you ever been an advocate for anyone? Have you ever spoken up on behalf of another person? Could you tell a story about that? Advocate stories are always fun to hear.

ALMIGHTY (all-MY-tee)   *Psalm 91:1—6*

Almighty! Now there's a word! We don't use that word too often. I can't really think of anything I've ever called "almighty" except God—and "the almighty dollar." Whenever we confess our faith in the words of the Apostles' Creed, we call God almighty. Find a copy of the Apostles' Creed and look for the word *almighty*. If you've memorized the Creed, count which word it is. Is it one? Four? Seven? Ten? Twenty-two? I think it's seven.

How mighty is almighty? Well, let's see.

Our almighty God has built a universe so large that if you could fly at the speed of light (186,000 miles per second), it would take you 1.3 seconds to get to the moon. That's a long distance! It would take you eight minutes to get to the sun. That's a longer distance! It would take you 33,000 years, flying at the speed of light, to get to the middle of the Milky Way. That's the kind of universe our almighty God laid out and in which He placed billions of stars and planets and other existing things. What's even more amazing is that beyond the reach of our largest telescope we know there is more. Now *that's* almighty!

But almighty also describes His ability to carefully review all the actions of every person. He does so instantaneously. That means fast. He hears each prayer of every yearning heart. He hears the prayer immediately. This almighty God has the whole world in His hands—just like the song says. Only an almighty God would have that.

Now let me tell you something exciting. One of our almighty God's names is Immanuel. Immanuel (sometimes spelled Emmanuel) means "God with us." Our Immanuel, our almighty God, is with us. More than that, He is for us. He showed He is for and with us when He sent His heart's desire, Jesus, to save us from our sins and earn salvation for us all.

Think of the most powerful force you can imagine. A hurricane? A tornado? The thrust of a spaceship's rockets? A nuclear explosion? The pounding tide or sweeping flood? All of those things are powerful, but they are as nothing compared to the might of our almighty God. Don't worry. We don't have to fear Him. He is our Friend. And if He is our Friend, what should we fear?

A wonderful man of faith, who trusted in an almighty God,

wrote Psalm 56:11. Look it up. Can you say that?

ALTAR (ALL-tur)   *Matthew 5:23–24*

No matter what yours looks like, and no matter where you place it in the church, when the people of God gather for worship, the altar is the center of attention. It should be. It represents three very important things in our worship life.

First, the altar reminds us of altars in the Old Testament. People brought sacrifices of valuable things in those days. They placed them on altars as a way of showing their commitment and loyalty to God. Sometimes they brought live animals. Sometimes grain. Sometimes other precious things. They wanted to give their best for the One who was best to them. But they couldn't outgive God. He gave the finest sacrificial gift ever, the Lamb of God—Jesus. He was the sacrifice for all the bad ever done, past, present, and future. Your church's altar keeps saying, "Christ died for you." Sad news. Glad news.

The altar also is to remind us of a tomb. It's supposed to look something like a cave—the cave in which Jesus was buried. But like Christ's burial cave, the altar is empty. There is nothing inside our altar. There was nobody in that burial cave of Jesus after Easter morning. Our altar reminds us that He rose, and that we will rise someday, too.

Finally, the altar looks like a table. Remember the table where Jesus sat with His disciples the Thursday evening before He died? He talked to them there about love; about being united with Him; about the new meaning He was giving to the eating of the Passover bread and drinking the Passover wine. The altar reminds us that we are at the table with the Savior, and each other, whenever we come for Communion. We are receiving again the true body and blood of the Lord, Jesus Christ.

Draw a picture of the most impressive altar you've ever seen. Were there words on it? Include them in your picture. Explain what you include.

If you're able, draw a floor plan of a church. Show where the altar is placed. Are there other places where it could be? Think about that.

AMEN (AH-MEN or AY-MEN)   *Nehemiah 8:6*

Right! You bet! For sure! Yes! I agree! You better believe it!

Wow! Terrific! Yeah, man! Hey, Hey! Right on! Out of sight! No question! You're correct! That's the way I feel! Count on me! My feelings exactly! No doubt!

Those are some of the things that *amen* means. Whether you pronounce it *ay*men or *ah*men doesn't make any difference. It's the same thing.

Saying amen is something like signing your name. When you sign your name to a paper or a contract, or even to a test, you are stating that you agree with what is written under, or before, your signature. Your signature is like an amen. Or maybe it's the other way around. Could it be that amen is like writing a big signature?

Sometimes we want to say an amen that is so big and so loud that the whole world will tilt and shake. It would if we could say it the way we feel!

Think about amen. Think about doing two things with your amen:

1. List as many things as you can think of to which we usually say amen. Hymns? The benediction? You list more.
2. Make a list of other ways that you might say amen. Then write some "amen" sentences. I'll make a couple of suggestions. How about this for an amen sentence: "Jesus is my friend." What do you say to that? _____ Or "Moms and dads are important." What do you say to that? ____Or "God still loves me even when I sin." What do you say to that? _____ Fill in your amen if you agree. Can you write some more amen sentences?

ANGEL (AIN-jell)   *Psalm 91:11*

How many angel names do you know? It seems to me the only ones that I'm really sure of are names like Michael and Gabriel. But there's got to be at least one named Fred or Charlie. How about some named Louise and Ellen? Since there are millions and millions of angels, there's got to be a Ricky, a Sarah, and a Dawn.

But it really doesn't make any difference what angels are named. Names are not most important. The important thing about angels is what they do. So, what do angels do?

One thing angels do is praise God. All the time. If that strikes you as an odd way of spending time, think about the things we "praise" all day long. Don't we praise things like television, ice cream, friends, pets, bicycles in our conversation all day long? And what else are TV commercials or newspaper ads other than praises of different products? Angels have only one "product." God. Since they have seen Him (and we haven't), they know what they're doing. They realize that God is praiseworthy. They know He is greater than any—and all—the things we spend time praising. They praise God.

Angels also serve God as messengers. The word *angel* actually means "messenger."

Do you like being a messenger? Most people do. When the teacher asks, "Nelda, would you ask the principal if our class can go outside?" Nelda dashes right down the hall, brings the message to the principal, and then zips right back with the answer to the class. It's fun being a messenger. God's angels have double fun. They are messengers and they praise.

Will we do angel-things? One angel-thing for sure! We will praise God. Forever. We don't know about the messengering. But in the meantime, we have a chance to do both those angel-things right here. We can praise Him. Now. We can be His messenger. Now. Think about/talk about how you can do both those things right now—where you are.

APOSTLE (Uh-POSS-sull)   *Luke 22:14*

Most of the time when the Bible uses the word *apostle*, it is referring to the first 12 followers of Jesus. Later, Paul's name was added to the list of apostles. He described himself as an exception to the rule (Galatians 1:1). The rule was that to be called an apostle, you had to have: (1) been called by God; (2) been a follower of Jesus from the beginning of His ministry to the end; and (3) seen the Resurrection. Only 12 fully fit that description. Do you know who they are? I'll give you a verse that will help you remember their names. You can sing this verse to the melody of "Jesus Loves Me." The chorus is

> Yes, Jesus called them,
> Yes, Jesus called them,
> Yes, Jesus called them,
> He called them one by one.

The first verse is this: Jesus called them one by one: Peter,

Andrew, James, and John. Next came Philip, Thomas, too, Matthew and Bartholomew.

The second verse starts: James the one they called the Less, Simon, also Thaddeus, Twelfth apostle Judas made, Jesus was by him betrayed. There they are. Twelve apostles. But don't forget Paul.

Knowing who the apostles were is nice. People like to have their names remembered. But more important than knowing names is knowing what apostles did. The very word, *apostle*, gives us a hint. Apostle is an old Greek word that means "someone who has been sent."

Before Christ was born, an "apostle" was the soldier a general sent out at the end of a battle to arrange for a truce. Later, the title came to mean any person who was sent to act on behalf of another person. An apostle became something like an ambassador, or a legal representative.

Christians understand that apostles were persons sent by God to announce the good news of salvation and eternal life through Jesus Christ. The apostles were sent to say that even when sinners shame themselves, or hurt others and disobey our Father, God has provided another chance in our great Redeemer. God hates sin and condemns it as wrong. But He loves sinners and wants each of us to be right with Him. Apostles were sent to say that.

Twelve apostles. Why don't you study them? Each apostle has a special symbol. See if you can find out about the symbol of each apostle and what it means. Maybe you'll want to make copies of those symbols and put them in your room. They make great art!

ASCENSION (uh-SEN-shun) *Ephesians 4:8*

God likes to do things differently. Human beings must say, "Everything that goes up will come down." That's absolutely true—for us. As long as we live in a world in which there is gravity, everything that goes up comes down. Even helium balloons finally come down. Earth-orbiting satellites come down, too. But with God, it is different. Since He made gravity, He can ignore it. He turned things around for His Son: "What goes down must come up."

Ascension (and the action word *ascend*) means "go up." You

ascend the stairs if you are going to the next floor. Right? A hot air balloon ascends when you let it loose. Mountain climbers ascend as they move toward the peak. Ascend means go up.

The ascension Christians talk about means that, and more. The ascension Christians talk about refers to that wonderful day when Jesus was with His disciples. He said good-bye and rose from their presence (He went up), disappearing from their sight up into the heavens. Why don't you read about that in Acts 1:6–11? Do it now.

Wasn't that something? It makes sense, at least to God's people. The Jesus who came down to be among us as a baby in Bethlehem returned to the place from which He came when His work was done.

The ascension of Christ stamps one big word over His work of salvation: COMPLETED. First, He was in heaven. He came down. He did His work. He went back to heaven again. He is there now. The ascension of Christ also sets the stage for something else; something just as dramatic and exciting. Christ will make the forth-and-back trip again. He is in heaven. He will come to earth. He will return to heaven—this time, with us. 1 Thessalonians 4:13–18 teaches us that the ascension will happen again. The trumpet of God will sound, and all those who love the Lord will return with Him to heaven.

The Christian church celebrates the ascension of Jesus every year. It always falls on the same day of the week. Can you figure out what day it is? I'll give you a hint. Acts 1:3 tells us that He ascended 40 days after Easter. Easter is always on a Sunday. Now figure out what day of the week would be 40 days after Easter Sunday. Write that day here: _____ . Did you write Thursday? You were right. But there's the "other" Ascension Day coming. For you and me. What day will that happen? Will it be Monday? Tuesday? Wednesday? Thursday or Friday? Saturday? Sunday? I wonder.

ASH WEDNESDAY   *Esther 4:1–3*

Ashes are what's left after the wood, or something else that's burnable, is consumed by fire. In the ancient world, the people took some of the ashes from their fire and put it in their hair or smeared it over their faces when they were sad. It was a way of showing mourning.

We don't smear ashes on ourselves when we mourn. Yet we have ways of showing sadness, too. Sometimes people hang a black cloth on their house when they are sad. Or they wrap a black band around their arm, or close their business for a day. That's how they show sadness.

The early church wanted a way to show sadness over the death of Jesus. They knew He died for their sins. The first thing they did was pick a specific day for recalling the death of Jesus. Do you know what it's called? G __ __ d F __ __ __ __ __ y.

Later, they decided to set aside a longer period of time for mourning. It started as two weeks and stretched into a much longer period. They called that longest period Lent. Do you know how long it lasts? See if you can choose the right answer: (a) 10 days, (b) 20 days, (c) 40 days.

If you chose 40 days, you chose right. Start with Easter and count backward 40 days. Don't count the Sundays. The Sundays are already set aside as our way of remembering the resurrection of Jesus. Sundays are not a part of Lent. When you count back 40 days from Easter, you will come to a Wednesday. That is the day Christians call Ash Wednesday.

The reason we call it Ash Wednesday is that early Christians would, on that day, take the palm branches that waved on Palm Sunday in the church the year before, burn them, and with the ashes from the palm branches, make a little mark on their foreheads. That mark was usally in the form of a cross. It was a way of remembering that Jesus died on the cross for them. It was a way of showing their sadness.

One of the strangest things about Lent and Ash Wednesday is that they stir up mixed feelings. Sad and glad. While on Ash Wednesday we are sad that Christ had to die, we are also glad that He was willing to do it for us. The "for us" are the important words. While we are sad that we sin, we are glad that God loves us so much that He wanted to forgive us. The "wanted to forgive us" is the important part in *that* sentence. See how sad/glad works?

Ash Wednesday is a sad/glad day. Which is it most for you? Sad? Glad? Talk about it a little bit.

ATONE (uh-TONE)   *Leviticus 17:11*
The day that Mr. Marks and Mr. Bryan had their big fight

was the day that Mr. Marks decided to build a fence. They didn't fight because he built the fence. He built the fence because they had a fight.

Mr. Marks and Mr. Bryan had been good neighbors. They had liked each other. But one day someone (Mr. Bryan thought it was Mr. Marks' dog) had trampled Mr. Bryan's flower bed. Soon after, someone (Mr. Marks thought it was the careless Bryan kids) threw a rock and cracked Mr. Marks' patio window. One harsh word led to another. One threat led to another. The next thing you knew an unnecessary fence was standing between their houses as a daily reminder of old hurts that could not be (or were not) overlooked.

What happened then? Christopher Christianson, a good friend of both Mr. Marks and Mr. Bryan, determined that it was time to get into the act. He talked with both of them. He helped Mr. Bryan see that while it could have been the Marks' dog that trampled his pretty flowers, he couldn't be sure.

And he helped Mr. Marks understand that anyone might have thrown a rock. There was no way of knowing whether the Bryan boy had done it.

Bit by bit, Mr. Bryan and Mr. Marks softened in their feelings toward each other. They recognized the need to straighten things out. Mr. Christianson helped there, too. He helped them apologize to each other.

The day they both met, mumbled an apology, shook hands, and promised to control their tempers was a great day. But the fence was still there. Mr. Christianson knew that as long as the fence was standing, the healing was not complete. Do you know what Mr. Christianson suggested? He said, "Split the cost of putting up the fence and tear it down." And that's what they did.

That little story hints at what the word "atone" means. Break the word in two pieces: *at* + *one*. Mr. Bryan and Mr. Marks were separated by their anger, but with the help of Mr. Christianson, they were made one in friendship again. There was an atonement.

In another and much more serious way, God and man (who were friends at the beginning) were separated by man's sin. Man did the hurting *and* built the fence. (Remember who was hiding from whom in the garden? Look it up in Genesis 3:9.)

But there was no outside friend to help mend things between God and man. God had to provide that. He sent His Son to destroy the separating "fence" and, by His death on the cross, join God and man in friendship again. Through Jesus, we are one with God. Jesus, God's Son, *atoned* for our sins.

Other words in this book will explain more about that rebuilding process. Right now, realize that you are *at-one* with God. Christ atoned for us.

B.

BAPTIZE (BAP-tize)   *Matthew 28:19*

Baptize? I'll tell you what it means. It means to apply water. You can do it a number of ways: by washing, by pouring, by sprinkling, or by immersing. Baptize means to apply water.

For Christians, baptize and Baptism means a lot more than getting people wet with either a little or a lot of water. That's why most Christians don't argue about how the water is applied in Baptism. They are more concerned with what's happening when the water (combined with the Word) touches the Christian.

So what *is* happening? By Baptism we are being combined with Christ. We are joined with all He did. We are born with Him. We live His life. We die His death. We are buried with Him. *And we rise with Him.* Finally, we will one day reign triumphantly with Him. All this is ours in Baptism. We "put on" Christ just as if He were a heavy fur coat on a cold, cold day. Check me out on that by reading Galatians 3:26–27 and Romans 6:3.

St. Peter (1 Peter 3:21) had another picture of what happens in Baptism. He sees the Baptism experience like a ship that's floating on the water. The water holds up the ship so that it always stays on top. If the level of the water goes up, the ship goes up, too. If the level drops, the ship drops with it. The water supports and protects the ship.

Baptism does that for us, too. Baptism is also a way of entering the family of faith. Acts 2:38 and so many other places underline that point. It makes us one with Christ *and with each other.*

There are many other wonderful things to understand about Baptism. But one more demands our recognition. It's simple, and yet it's complicated. Some people think that Baptism is something we do for God. The truth is just the opposite. Baptism is something God does for us. It is the washing of regeneration and the renewing *of the Holy Spirit* (Titus 3:5). It's God's work. Because Baptism is God's work, we treasure it in a special way. You and I ought to know some things that took place when we were baptized. Let's see what you know:

1. Where were you baptized? Can you list the place—the building, the city, and the state?

2. Who had the honor of baptizing you into the Christian faith?

3. One more thing. What was the date of your baptism?

Next year, why not celebrate your *two* birthdays: Why not celebrate the day on which you were born and the day on which you were reborn through Baptism? What do you think you could do on your baptism birthday that would make it special?

BELIEVE (buh-LEAVE)   *Acts 16:31*

A lot of the words we use in the church don't sound alike but seem to mean the same thing. Believe is one of those words. Can you tell me the difference between believe and faith? I have trouble until I unravel those words a little bit. Then the differences are clearer. Here's the way I make the difference between believe and faith.

Believe is the verb (an action word), while faith is a noun (the name of a person, place, or thing). When you have *faith* (the name of a thing), you *believe* (an action). I can shorten it even more. I can say,"Faith is action." Or I can say,"Believe is faith with its sleeves rolled up."

The Bible says that Abraham believed in the Lord (Genesis 15:6). Since believe is an action, he must have done something. When you read his life story, you realize that Abraham did a lot of things because He believed in the Lord. He left his home-land. He trusted he would have a son, even though it took so long. After the son was born, he was willing to sacrifice the son at God's request. He did all this because he believed in God. He acted. Because he was sure God would keep His word, would provide protection, would lead him in the proper ways, he acted. Abraham believed, and he acted.

Many years later, another man believed through action: A prison warden came to his jail and found all the doors wide open. He thought every prisoner had escaped. He was so upset that he tried to kill himself. One of the prisoners stopped him. The story of all that is told in Acts: 16:25–34. Read that section and find the name of the man who told the jailer not to kill himself. Write that name here: _____.

Did you write Paul? Correct.

But that's not the end of the story. Look at the question the jailer asked. Then look at the answer Paul gave: "*Believe* in the Lord Jesus." Now go back to the story one more time. Read it again. This time, make a list of the actions that took place because the jailer believed.

My list looks like this:

1. The jailer listened to Paul tell about Jesus.
2. The jailer brought other members of his family to hear.
3. The jailer cleaned Paul's wounds.
4. The jailer acted immediately.
5. The jailer brought him to his own home.
6. The jailer fed Paul.
7. The jailer was baptized together with his whole household.
8. The jailer rejoiced.

Those eight actions all happened because of one word: *believe*. When the jailer believed, he did all those things.

Believe sounds like a powerful word to me. Could you think of eight things people do today because they believe in Jesus Christ?

BENEDICTION (ben-uh-DIK-shun)   *Genesis 48:8–10*

Many of our English church words come from a language called Latin. If you know a little Latin, you can figure out many English words. Let me show you.

Benediction is an English word based on two Latin words.

The two Latin words are hooked together. The first Latin word (*bene*) means good. The second word (*diction*) means speak. Now tie the two together. What do you get?

If you say that *bene-diction* means speak good, or good speech, or a good word, or something like that, you are correct. It is a blessing, or a wish for the best directed toward someone.

There are a lot of benedictions in our life. Can you think of some? How about this one: "Have a good time!" That's a benediction. Or how about "I hope everything works out okay," or "Good health and a safe trip." Those are benedictions.

There are two great benedictions used in the church. They are usually said at the end of the worship service as people prepare to leave. The last thing we want them to hear as they walk out the door is a good word. One of these benedictions is called the Aaronic (ay-ur-RON-ik) benediction. It gets its name from Aaron, who first spoke it in Numbers 6:24–26. The other benediction is called the Pauline (paw-LEEN) benediction, because it was given to us by St. Paul. One version of that benediction is in 2 Corinthians 13:14.

Find the Aaronic benediction and write it here:

_____

_____

_____

Now find the Pauline benediction in 2 Corinthians 13:14, and write it here:

_____

_____

_____

Do you think you could write a benediction? Try it. Write it here:

_____

_____

_____

BIBLE (BUY-bul)   *John 5:39*

Our word *bible* is not in the Bible. But what the word *bible* describes is all through the Bible. Is that hard to understand? Maybe. Let's see if we can unscramble it.

Guess what the word *bible* means. Pick an answer. Bible means: (a) a little bib; (b) wisdom; (c) book; (d) two.

If you guessed a, b, or d, you are not correct. C is the right answer. Bible means book. Just as simple as that: book.

When the early Christians were looking for a word to give their collection of holy writings, they chose the simplest and least complicated word they could find. They called it the book. The Bible. For them, their holy writings was *the book. The Bible.* What do you know about the Book? Let me check you out. (1) The Bible is divided into two/three/four/eight major sections. (2) [T F] Each section has a name. (3) One section is called the _ _ _ Testament. (4) Another section is called the _ _ _ Testament. (5) All the individual books in the _ _ _ Testament were written before Christ was born. (6) Altogether, there are _ _ individual books in the Bible.

How did you do? The correct answers are *2, true, old, new, old, 66.*

In general, if you want to know about what happened from the beginning of the world until the time of Moses, you will find all that in the Book of Genesis. If you want to read about things that happened to the Lord Jesus during His life, you would read Matthew, Mark, Luke, John, or the first chapter of Acts. The Psalms are wonderful poetry, and Proverbs has great advice for life. Esther is an adventure story. Revelation gives us a view of heaven and what takes place there. Each part of the Bible has a specific flavor to it.

As great as what I have told you about specific books of the Bible, the real purpose of the Bible is explained in 2 Timothy 3:15. Complete Paul's explanatory words about the Bible, which he says is able to make you " w _ _ _ u _ _ _ s _ _ _ _ _ _ _ _ t _ _ _ _ _ _ f _ _ _ _ i _ C _ _ _ _ _ _ J _ _ _ _ _ " (KJV). The next two verses (16 and 17) teach us that the Bible is also intended to train us for Christian living.

I haven't told you nearly all there is to know about the Bible. You'll keep on learning more about it the rest of your life. But one additional exciting truth about the Bible is Psalm 119:105. Draw a picture that explains the meaning of that verse.

CALL/CALLED   *1 Corinthians 1:1–2*

"Did you hear, Billy? Did you hear?" asked Fred.

"Hear what?" responded Billy to his friend.

"Our congregation called a pastor last night. He now lives in Arizona. We want him to come be with us. We want him to be our leader. We called him," said Fred.

"Called? What do you mean, called? You mean someone made a long-distance phone call to him and asked him to come? Is that what you mean?" Billy asked.

"Oh, no. That's not what called means to us. I suppose someone did phone him. But when we say we called a pastor, we mean that we chose him to be our spiritual leader and friend. We looked over the names of a lot of pastors we might have asked. We prayed. Then the congregation voted. We believe that our choice was God's choice. So we sent him a call."

Billy wasn't all that impressed by Fred's explanation. He still didn't really know what Fred was so excited about. But people who use the word *called* like Fred used it, and who believe that God calls men and women to serve in His church get very excited about a call. They are convinced that God called people to faith and service through the Gospel in the past. They believe He calls His own from the darkness of unbelief to the light of His love today. They know He still calls some to full-time service, for Him, in His church.

When the process of selecting a pastor or other servant is spiritual, we say that the pastor is *called;* that the teacher chosen is *called;* that the deaconess is *called;* that the lay-worker, as well as any other who has been selected for full-time service, is *called.*

Find out how *calls* are made in your congregation. Who does the calling? How is it done? See if you can look at the piece of paper that is sent to the person called. Ask your pastor or teacher whether you could see their *call.* Ask them to tell you how they were called to your congregation and how they decided to come. Ask them what they think about being called and what it means to them. You might be surprised by their answers.

CANDLES   *John 1:4*

Candles have always been an important part of worship to God's people, whether in the Old Testament or the New. Were candles important because they gave light? Or did they use candles as a symbol? (Did you know that you can see a candle for miles on a dark night? Knowing that, can you figure out a symbolical meaning of candles?)

There's more to be known about candles. Candles not only give light—they give heat. Candles can warm things. A candle burning in a snowbound automobile during subfreezing weather gives off enough heat so that people in the car won't freeze. They may be very cold, but they won't freeze.

Whether candles were used in the church because of the light or the heat, candles have been an important part of worship for many centuries.

I suppose the first candles were placed on or beside the altar to help the worship leader see what he was doing. Make sense? After a while, people began to use the number of candles burning as a reminder of other things.

One candle makes them think of Jesus. Many churches still have a paschal (PASS-kul) candle, which reminds us of Jesus, the Good Shepherd and Lord. Sometimes the paschal candle is lit the Saturday before Easter and then burns until Ascension Day. In other instances, it is lit on Epiphany (Jan. 6) and burns until Ascension Day, when it is put out as the congregation says in the creed, " . . . He ascended into heaven."

If the paschal candle burns from Epiphany to Ascension Day, it is to remind us that Christ is "a Light to lighten the Gentiles" (Luke 2:32 KJV). If it burns from Easter Eve on, it is to remind us of the 40 days Jesus walked on the earth after His resurrection before he returned to His Father's home.

Two candles made people think of Jesus' divine and human natures. He was true God and true man.

Six burning candles remind us of the days of creation.

Seven was a sacred number in the Old Testament and symbolizes completion.

Now you think a little bit. What might 10 candles mean? Or

12? Regardless of how many candles used, the important thing is what the candles teach.

When I look at candles, I remember two great things Jesus said about light. He said, "I am the Light of the world" (John 8:12). He also said, "You are the light of the world" (Matthew 5:14). He is the Light. We are the light. When He shines in our lives, He brightens us and makes us shiny, too.

But what about you. What meaning does the burning candle bring to your mind? Draw a candle. Either draw things around your candle that a candle brings to your mind or clip photos from magazines and paste them around the candle to show your thoughts. Let your picture selections tell what a candle in church means to you.

CATHOLIC (KATH-o-lik)   *Ephesians 3:15*

When some people confess the Apostles' Creed, they say, "I believe in the holy *Christian* church, the communion of saints, the forgiveness of sins . . ." When others confess the same creed, they say, "I believe in the holy *catholic* church, the communion of saints . . ." See the difference? Why do some say catholic and some say Christian?

The oldest way of saying the creed is, "I believe in the holy catholic church." The word *catholic* actually means "whole" or "entire." By that word the early Christian church wanted to say that it believed there was a great unity in the Christian faith. They felt it was a unity greater than that of any one congregation or church. For them the church leaped the boundaries of nations and was not restricted by time. They believed Jesus united *all* Christians who had *ever* lived anywhere in the world. The word *catholic* was their gathering word. It was a claiming word. It included. It said, "We are one in Christ. We are one with each other."

Later, because people thought that the phrase "holy catholic church" meant the Roman Catholic Church (a worldwide denomination with headquarters in Rome, Italy, and supervised by its leader, the pope), many early Protestants substituted the word *Christian* for the word *catholic*. It's not a bad switch. Nor is it an improper switch. But it's not quite the match of the word *catholic*. It doesn't mean exactly the same thing. If it did, I wouldn't have to write this much of an explanation.

The next time you confess the Apostles' Creed, stop at the phrase, "The holy *Christian/catholic* church." Try out some other words in that place. See if you can find one or more words that picture for you a gathering of all Christians who have ever lived or who ever will live from every corner of the world. Picture a gathered, united, entire, whole people. They are what catholic means. Can you find another word for that?

CHANCEL (CHAN-cel)   *Exodus 26:31-35*

Chancel almost sounds like cancel. One way I have for re-membering what a chancel is is by thinking about the word *cancel.*

When you cancel something, you cross it off. You act like it doesn't exist anymore. A bank cancels a check when the money has been paid. They stamp it "paid." That check can't be used again. Ask your mom or dad to show you a canceled check. Let them explain what happens to the check between the time they write it and the time it came back to them "canceled."

The chancel is an area in the church where Christian can-celing takes place. Things are stamped "paid." Things like sin. Specifically the chancel is the area between the Communion rail and the altar. If your church doesn't have a Communion rail, it's the area around the altar where high and holy things take place. You know what those are!

When I think of high and holy things, I think of Baptism—for example. Remember what gets canceled in Baptism? The Bible is read in that high and holy place. The Bible is powerful. It brings us the One who cancels sin, Jesus Christ. In many churches, our high and holy Lord's Supper is presented from the edge of the chancel at the Communion rail. In other churches that Sacrament is distributed within the chancel it-self.

The word *chancel* means "bars," or a "fence." In the early church, some Christians built a kind of fence around the altar area to keep the wrong people from entering the place where they thought only a pastor should go. Today we don't worry much about that. We don't call it a chancel because we want to keep the common people out. We call it the chancel because it marks the area where God speaks clear, canceling words to His folks. We call it the chancel as a reminder that the altar is the area where some powerful and important things take place.

Look back at the sketch you made when we talked about the altar. Draw the chancel area around the altar. Mark it.

Next time you go into your church, look at the chancel. Think of the wonderful things that happen there. One way to always remember the specialness of the chancel area is to recall all the things that we cancel in the chancel.

CHOSEN   *1 Peter 2:9*

Rick hated some recesses. He didn't hate all recesses. He just hated those when they played baseball. That meant choosing sides. He hated those ball-playing recesses because, when the choosing of sides was over, he was always the last one. He never really got picked. He just ended up on the team that was unlucky enough to have the last choice.

There had been some embarrasing baseball days last year. Team captains had actually argued whether they had to take him or not. They said hurtful things like, "That's okay, you can have him. Put him somewhere in the infield and maybe a ball will bounce off of him." Rick hated that kind of talk. He just hated it. He dreamed of the day when someone, somewhere, would actually choose him. But that wasn't likely on baseball days.

I don't know many things in the Bible that are more exciting than reading about God choosing. He actually chooses those who will believe. Did you know that? If you believe and trust that Christ is your Savior, if you are convinced that God has set aside a special place in eternity for you, the reason is that God has chosen you and has given you the faith needed to believe. Your proof that you have been chosen is your faith.

People who have faith are chosen people. People who are chosen have faith. It works both ways. If you believe that God has sent Jesus Christ for you, then you can believe something else, too. You can believe that God chose you.

Check your life. Are there parts of it that show the world you know you are chosen? Finish this sentence: "Because I know that God has chosen me, I—" Finish it three ways. Can you? Sure you can. Let me give you some help. What do you do because you know that God has chosen you? One thing I do is pray. Do you? Worship? Love? What else?

CHRIST   *John 4:25*

The first thing you need to know about the word *Christ* is that it is not a name. Christ is a title. It's like Mr. Rogers, engineer. Mr. Rogers is a name. Engineer is his title. Saying Jesus Christ is like saying Mr. Black, the principal; Mr. Wills, the policeman; Mrs. Barr, the nurse. Jesus was His name. Christ was His title. That fact is clearest when we call Him *Jesus, the Christ.*

Christ is the same word in Greek that *messiah* is in Hebrew. Christ = Messiah. Since part of our Bible was written in Hebrew and part of it in Greek, it's natural that both words appear. The word *messiah* appears in both the Old and New Testaments. The word *christ* is used only in the New Testament. Both of these words mean the same thing. They mean "the anointed one." But what does that mean?

Long ago, when a king or other special leader was chosen, he would be anointed. This was usually done by one of God's holy men. When the king was anointed, a little oil was poured on his head in public. And then the holy man would say out loud that the anointed one would be king, special leader. That's how people knew who was to rule next. Or lead. He was anointed.

Does that sound odd? Does pouring oil on someone's head seem strange? Think about it. Don't we do the same thing? Not with oil. With water. Is there a time when water is poured on someone's head? In church? Doesn't that "anointing" show that the person is set aside as a child of God. Do you know what I'm talking about? Baptism, of course. When we are baptized, water is poured on our head. We are anointed and given a special title. After we are anointed, we are called the redeemed of God; His children; believers; and many other wonderful titles.

Being anointed the Messiah, or the Christ, is not exactly the same as being baptized. But it's similar. The Christ, or the Messiah, was selected to be God's special King who would first give His life and then, by the giving, save the world. He is to finally rule over everything.

Only one was anointed as the Christ. That Anointed One was Jesus. That is why He is called Jesus, the Christ, and Jesus, the Messiah. He was anointed to be Savior, God, and Lord.

CHRISTMAS   *Luke 2:1–7*

Christmas. Now there's a happy word! I wonder what you know about Christmas. Let's see. Try these true and false questions.

1. T   F   Christmas is the oldest Christian festival.
2. T   F   Christmas was started by Santa Claus
3. T   F   Christmas isn't very important to Christians.

Did you answer all those questions false? If you did, you are correct. Christmas is *not* the oldest festival. Easter is. Christians remembered Easter because that was the day Christ rose from the dead. That was the first festival. Christians remember Christmas because Christ came into the world to be just like us, so that by His work He could save us. Easter was considered more important by the early Christians. What do you think about that?

Santa Claus doesn't have a lot to do with Christian Christmas. Why should we fuss with that jolly little man in a red suit when we have an exciting great God who loves us and gives us more than Santa ever could? Santa is often part of another kind of Christmas. That other Christmas has little to do with the Savior. Christians have a good time with their Christmas even without a Santa. No, Christmas wasn't started by Santa Claus. The answer to the second questions is false.

And, finally, Christians believe Christmas is extremely important. It celebrates the great visible action of God, who sent a real baby for us. God planned to rescue all people from sin and Satan through that baby. Christmas is very important. The answer to the third questions is false.

There are a lot of Christmas customs that can help us understand Christmas better. How about this one: Christmas trees. Christmas trees are green and live to remind us that our life in Christ is fresh, green, and living. Did you know that?

And the ornaments on the tree are to remind us of the gifts which the _ _ _ _   _ _ _ brought (Matthew 2:11). The lights? They are to remind us of Christ who is the " _ _ _ _ _ of the world" (John 8:12). The gifts we give each other bring to mind the great Gift that Jesus is for us. Can you think of other things that remind us of the true meaning of Christmas?

CHURCH   *Colossians 1:18*

"Let's have a contest," said Craig. "Let's see who can draw the best church." With that, the whole class buckled down to the challenge. All took paper. Some took crayons. Some had pens. Other picked up pencils. A scissors started working here and there. Everyone was busy trying to draw, or construct, a church.

Craig drew a big white building with a white steeple and a cross at the highest point. At the bottom of his paper, he wrote *"Trinity Lutheran Church."* A lot of other kids drew pictures like his.

Mary's picture was different. It was a skyscraper. It had a lot of windows. Flags flew from the top. By the fancy front door, she wrote the words, *"The Lutheran Building."* That was where her father worked as a mission planner for the Lutheran Church. Her sign said "church." It must be a church. In her mind a church was an organization that had a big office building filled with people who worked all over the world.

Leo drew the strangest picture. He just drew people. All kinds of stick people. Some were men. Some were women. Some were children. Two or three had beards. One had a cane. He drew people. When the teacher asked him what his drawing means, Leo answered, "My pastor told me that the church is people who love Jesus. So I drew people. All kinds of people."

Who do you think drew the correct picture? Craig? Mary? Leo? The answer is all of them. Each picture is correct in its own way.

The word *church* can refer to a church building like the one in which you worship. Church can also mean an organization doing God's work all over the world. And, of course, church always means people. Even though you don't worship in a church building, or maybe you don't belong to a worldwide church organization, you can still have a church if you have people. As a matter of fact, you can't have a church without people.

Look through some magazines or newspapers. Find pictures that can illustrate each of these three things that church means. Or maybe you'd like to try to duplicate the drawings of Craig, Mary, and Leo.

COLLECT (CALL-lekt)   *Jonah 2:1*

Some words used in the church can really confuse. They look alike. They may even sound similar. But that's where comparisons end. Here's two such words: *collect* and *collection*. What's the difference?

Collection is a gathering of money or gifts. Most Christians call that an offering. It makes a difference whether we are "collecting" for God or whether we are "offering" our expressions of thanksgiving and praise. But, at the same time, if you say, "We're going to have a collection," folks know what you mean. A *collect*? That's different. It sounds different, with the accent on the first syllable. Compare the two of them. Call-lect. Collect-tion. See? They do sound different. Most of all, they are different.

A collect is a special prayer. It is special because someone has worked very hard to gather important thoughts in simple language. Collects often sound like poetry. They are brief. They seldom contain more than 10 lines. Some have less than that.

Each Sunday of the year has its own collect. The collect is based on the thought of the Scripture reading for that day. In addition, there are other collects—prayers—for the church, for peace, for the Word, for many other special things. Page around in the front of the hymnbook. See if you can't find some collects.

While we're at it, why don't we write a collect. I'll give you a subject. You prepare the collect.

First, some instructions. A collect has three parts:
1. Name God as the subject ("O blessed Father in heaven . . .")
2. Express your request. Clearly. Briefly.
3. Attach an ending ("through Jesus Christ, our Lord . . .")

Now, you try it. Write a collect about the family. Or maybe about your congregation. What about one for missionaries?

COMFORTER (CUM-for-tur)   *John 14:26*

It's really great living in this last part of the 20th century. There are so many wonderful things available to us now. TV. Cars. Telephones. Snowmobiles. Popsicles. But don't think that yesterday was without its pleasure and fun, too! Yesterday they had something called a comforter.

When I was a boy, almost every bed had a big warm fluffy feather-filled cover that was light as a breeze and warm as an oven. They were put on the beds during the cold part of the year. They were called comforters. Since most bedrooms were not heated (would you believe that?), boys and girls getting ready for bed would undress in the bathroom around a small stove, put on their PJs, and dash to the bed. As soon as they hit the bed, they pulled the comforter over them—as fast as they could.

For a few seconds, the chill would grip. Then the warmth and softness of the comforter settled in. Snuggled there in that pocket of protection, sleep came quickly. We were comforted by the comforter. People called it a comforter because it was such a comfort.

The Scripture talks about a Comforter, too. That Comforter is not a warm blanket. The Comforter in Scripture is the Holy Spirit, whom Jesus promised to send to His followers. He promised the Comforter. He kept the promise. He still keeps it.

What does the Comforter do? The Comforter gives the same sense of warmth, security, and protection that my feather blanket did. Only more. He brings the warmth of faith, the security of forgiveness, the protection of grace, and the joy of salvation. Those things make you feel different. They make you feel great.

Sometime, when you think about the Holy Spirit, imagine a huge warm blanket wrapped around you on a cold and stormy night. That's what He's like.

God wants you to have that special Comforter. He sends that Comforter to us in so many wonderful ways. He sends the Comforter through Baptism, the Lord's Supper, and through the Word.

The Comforter is coming. For you.

COMMUNE (kuh-MYOON)   *1 Corinthians 12:12–13*
One of the reasons we can have so much fun with our "church words" is that each one was selected by the early Christians to describe something in their faith. But that word had meaning before the Christians picked it. For example, people knew about sons before Christ was called the Son of God. And people talked about lights and truth before these titles were attached to our Lord.

Knowing what a word meant before it was selected by Christians can help us understand exactly what the church word is to mean now. Take the word *commune*, for example.

Commune, long ago, meant "to share, or have something in common." It meant that before people started using it in the Christian church. And now?

On those great summer days, when you lie on your back in the grass, watching the clouds and the birds and the trees and feeling the breeze, you can say, "I am communing with nature." You are united with all creation. You have feelings in common with the whole world.

In the church, the word *commune* is used to describe what happens when people kneel at the edge of the chancel and receive the Lord's Supper. Their identical experience (all are at the same place, have the same faith, and are receiving the same gift of God) is called communing.

Look again at commune. Look carefully. Change the fifth letter and drop the last. What do you have? *Common*. Commune means to have something in common.

I'm going to write three sentences using commune. All of them are true. Figure out why.

1. All fourth-graders commune in class.
2. Members of my family commune at home.
3. Because of our friendship, my friends and I commune when we play.

Do you understand that word now? Do you understand that commune means most of all that you are sharing something in common with someone or something. Now let's see you make a couple of sentences with the word *commune*. It won't be easy, but you can do it.

COMMUNICANT (Kuh-MYOO-ni-kuhnt) *1 Corinthians 12:14*

Now there's a word you don't run into everyday! *Communicant*. It's not very common. Yet when you think about it, it's more common that it first appears. Communicant has much in common with commune.

The simplest way I can explain communicant is this: people who commune are communicants. Or turn it around: people who are communicants commune. They share something special together.

When Christians use the term communicant, they usually mean those people who share their faith and who participate in the Lord's Supper with them. It's like we said: communicants commune together.

But the word is used in another way, too. The word *communicant* is used to describe the individual member of a church or a denomination. A congregation is said to have 273 communicants. Or a Lutheran Church body has 1,988,000 communicant members. Another meaning of communicant is someone who is recognized as an official member of a church body, whether a congregation or a national organization.

How do people become communicants? What steps do they take? Ask someone in your church that question. Find out how to become a communicant in your congregation.

And while we're at it, why don't you find you how many communicant members there are in your congregation. Put the number here: _____.

Finally, there are things which a communicant member will want to do. I have made a list of things I believe a communicant member does. Circle the answers you think are wrong. A communicant member will (1) worship each week; (2) pray for other members in the church; (3) have their children baptized; (4) receive the Lord's Supper regularly; (5) bring offerings; (6) help fellow members in need.

I think those are all things a communicant would do. What do you think?

COMMUNION (kuh-MYOON-yun)   *1 Corinthians 11:23–26*
We've had commune. We've had communicant. Now we're ready for this sentence: *Communion* is when a communicant communes.

Communion has other names in the church. Some call it the Lord's Supper. Some call it the Sacrament of the Altar. Some call it the Holy Eucharist (YOU-kah-rist). Those first two names are obvious. But what about the last?

Eucharist means thanksgiving or gratitude. What a good name for Communion! Communion is a time we give thanks and are grateful for the gift of Jesus. By whatever name you call it, all those words refer to when members of a Chrisitian congregation receive, together, the precious body and blood of our Lord, Jesus Christ. It comes in and with bread and wine. We believe it is actually and truly the body and blood of the

Savior. In Communion, Christ becomes part of us (wonder of wonders!), and we become part of Him. A further blessing is that when we commune with others, we become a part of them, too!

Does this all sound strange? When the early Romans were told that Christians communed, they thought Christians were cannibals. They heard about eating and drinking the body and blood. They thought Christians were eating each other. Communion is always hard to explain to people who doesn't recognize the Lord Jesus or realize the miracle of Communion. How can you explain the fact that Jesus is truly present "in, with, and under the bread and the wine" to those who have no faith?

But we need to say that we eat and drink Christ in a different way than other eating and drinking. Christ is truly present in the bread and wine through eyes of faith. If we believe that we receive Him, we do receive Him. In receiving Him, we also receive everything He did for us. He (we) overcame Satan. He (we) satisfied the penalty of sin. He (we) defeated death and gained eternal life. All those things become ours through Communion.

You really ought to discover as much as you can about Communion. Why don't you find out how often Communion is available at your congregation? Put the number of times per month here: _____ .

While you're at it, how often do you think a Christian communicant ought to commune? And what should you do to get ready for Communion? Look around for answers to those questions in yourself, or in the Catechism, or in the front of a hymnbook. Best of all, "search the Scriptures."

Communion. Communion is when communicants commune. Right?

CONDEMN (kun-DEM)   *John 3:18*
Condemn is not a happy word. It doesn't even sound happy. It sounds heavy and troubled.

Condemn happens when someone did something wrong. Or if they didn't actually do the wrong, at least there were people who thought they did. Condemned people have been caught and blamed. It also means that some punishment has been assigned to them.

I can think of three things that are condemned in our world. Condemned murderers are taken to prison and sometimes put in a cell on death row. Condemned food is stored separately, marked "unfit for human use," and finally thrown away or destroyed. Condemned buildings are torn down or burnt to the ground. Condemn is a harsh word.

One of the many reasons Christians get so excited about Jesus Christ is that, because of Him, we are not condemned. We should be. We have sinned. We keep on sinning. Without Christ, we would all finally face the Judge, hear His words—"You are condemned"—and head off for punishment.

Farther on in this book, we will talk more about the how and why of condemning. We'll read about words like *sin* and *trespass* and even *damn*. We'll study God's holy will and His hopes for all people. How often we fail! We'll consider our failure to follow the intention of God. All put together, it doesn't make a very nice story. But it is true—from start to finish. The most important thing about all these words is that, as we study them, we learn how God provided a way to spare us. We need not die.

To prove you really understand the word *condemn*, see if you can find a story in your newspaper about someone or something condemned. That should be easy. If you have trouble, ask others in your family to help. If they ask why you want the help, you'll get a chance to tell them about the word *condemn*, too. But don't stop there. Be sure you say out loud, "Don't worry, though. People who trust in Jesus are not condemned. They are forgiven and kept for heaven." Be sure you say that.

CONFESS (kun-FESS)   *Matthew 10:32*

Do you know what a homonym is? A homonym is a word that sounds like another word with a different spelling and a different meaning. Like bear and bare. Those are homonyms. Or bow and bough. Or knight and night. Or here and hear. Or there and their. Those are all homonyms.

Confess is one word that has two separate meanings. It's almost a homonym. Remember that there are also words that are spelled the same but have different meanings. Confess is a word like that.

First of all, confess means to admit you did something wrong. When a store is robbed and the police catch a person, and that person admits to robbing the store, we say he confessed.

Or if Kurt cheats on a test and later tells the teacher what he did, she could say, "Kurt confessed to cheating on the spelling test. I'm glad he confessed."

Confess can mean that you admit you did something wrong. For Christians, confession leads to hearing the good news that Christ has forgiven all people who confess their sins.

But confess can also mean something else. It can mean making a public statement of what you believe. You can do it by voice. You can do it in writing. Christian confess their faith every Sunday morning (and often in between) when they say, out loud, one of the creeds. They are telling other people what they believe is correct.

Christians also confess in simpler ways. They confess when they let others know they trust Jesus, or that they are sure God has a place for them in heaven. When they say things like that, they are confessing.

All your life you will have chances to confess your faith. Time after time the moment will come when you can say what is important to you. Why not get ready for your chances right now. What are the three most important things you are willing to confess concerning your faith? You don't have to write them down. But be sure you have them in your mind, ready when someone like me asks.

CONSCIENCE (KON-shunts)   *1 Peter 3:16*

A conscience is the little voice inside your head (or that's where it sounds like it's coming from) that tells you when you are thinking or doing something wrong. It can say, "You shouldn't do that." But that's not all. It can also say, "You really *ought* to do that" when you are considering doing something that is right. It works both ways. Let me tell you a conscience story. Mark was out on the playground after school, just walking around, when he saw something green fluttering at his feet. He reached down and picked it up. A dollar bill! Wow!

He was all set to head for the drug store when a thought struck him. Lee had lost a dollar during recess. Mark heard Lee tell the teacher about losing a dollar. Lee had saved it to buy his mom a birthday present. But he lost it. As Mark thought about Lee's loss, he didn't know what to do. On the one hand, he could almost taste the sundae. On the other hand, he heard that inner voice saying he ought to tell the teacher what he found. What do you think Mark should do?

Well, Mark told the teacher. She said she would talk to Lee and find out whether he had found his dollar. She said she wasn't even sure Lee had lost a dollar bill. Maybe it was a dollar in change. She couldn't even remember for sure whether Lee had lost the dollar at school. She told Mark she would return the dollar to him if she wasn't sure it was Lee's.

Later, when Mark told the story to his pal. Mike, he got a surprising response. Mike laughed. "What a dope!" Mike said. "You should have kept the dollar. What do you care about Lee? If he's dumb enough to lose his money, that's his fault."

Mark told Mike about the voice inside, his conscience. Mike said, "Yeah, I hear that voice, too, sometimes. I ignore it."

Whether you obey that voice or ignore it, you have to deal with it. If you listen to it and do what it tells you, your conscience remains bright and alive. If you ignore it and trample all over it, your conscience gets weaker and weaker, until, in some people, it dies. Then you have no clear voice to keep you on the right path.

Whenever our conscience is getting weaker—or just a little confused—we can always strengthen it by seeking guidance from Scripture. Scripture strenthens a weak conscience. A good conscience that is constantly strengthened by the Word of God is a powerful force.

CONTRITE (kon-TRITE)   *Psalm 34:18*

You could tell by the look on his face just how very sorry Donnie was. Katie was lying on the ground crying. Her knee was badly scraped. It oozed blood. She was hurt. Donnie wasn't hurt—at least not on the outside. But on the inside, he ached. He knew he was responsible for what had happened.

He was just going to surprise Katie. He was hiding behind a bush and jumped out when Katie rode by on her bike. He thought he would scare her a little. He sure did. A lot!

When Donnie jumped, Katie lost control, wobbled off the sidewalk, hit a tree, and crashed to the ground. That wasn't really what Donnie had planned. He thought she'd just yelp and get mad. He didn't want to hurt her. He was so sorry for what he did. He was contrite.

A person who is contrite aches with regret. Contrition makes your heart feel like a big rock that has just been smashed—pounded—into a pile of gravel. A contrite person is so-o-o-o sorry.

The nicest thing about being so-o-o-o sorry is that you are then ready to receive forgiveness. You are ready. Right then. We'll talk more about that wonderful word, *forgiveness*, later. Right now, it's enough to know forgiveness is special first-aid cream for any hurting heart. It never stings, never sticks, and never hurts. It heals. It's best when it comes from God, but it's also okay when it comes from others! But remember this: forgiveness flows to contrition.

Katie finally stopped crying. Her aching knee kept hurting, but it did stop oozing. Donnie helped her up. He picked up her bike and walked toward home beside Katie. That's when Katie said some powerful words to a contrite Donnie. She said, "Donnie, I know you didn't want me to get hurt. And I don't think my knee hurts nearly as much as you do. Thanks for helping me home. Let's still be friends."

Donnie smiled. He wasn't contrite on the outside anymore. Even though he would feel strange in his heart for a long time, the soothing salve of forgiveness was working its wonder on his contrite attitude.

COVENANT (KUH-veh-nunt)   *Jeremiah 31:31–34*

A covenant is an agreement. That's the simplest definition I can give. A covenant is an agreement between at least two parties.

When your class decides to have a Halloween party and everyone agrees to bring food and help decorate the room, you have all made a kind of covenant. The covenant is an agreement between people agreeing to do something.

But sometimes people don't keep their agreement. They don't do what they promised to do. Instead, they whine about how hard the covenant is, or that others aren't doing their share. No matter the reason, sometimes people don't do what they agreed to do. Then the covenant is broken.

Covenant is a B-I-I-I-G Bible word. It's bigger than an agreement between students about a class party. It's bigger because one of those who share in a covenant agreement is God. The word *covenant* in the Bible always includes God. And when you're talking about a covenant and God, you need to know that He always keeps His promises. He does not fail to fulfill all He says He will do.

Where do you find a covenant in Scripture? One of the first covenants is in Genesis 3:15. There God promised Adam and Eve He would send a Savior.

Later, God made a covenant with Abraham. He said He would watch over Abraham and all of his grandchildren for many generations. He pledged to bless the whole world through Abraham's descendants. We know that Abraham's greatest grandson, many years after Abraham's death, was Jesus Christ.

The Old Testament is the story of God's covenant. He kept His promises and urged His followers to do the same. When they failed, He gave them another chance. And another. And still another. That covenant of God reached its peak in Jesus Christ. Read John 3:16. That verse is the covenant fulfilled.

I wish I could tell you that the people of God in all history always kept their side of their agreements. They didn't. The good news in the Bible is that when they broke the covenant, but asked for help, God forgave them. He still forgives all who fail in their part of the covenant and gives that forgiveness to them who ask. The covenant that He will be our God is still active for us today. His promise of life eternal for those who lean upon Him is as strong today as the first time He gave it. His covenant endures forever.

The word *covenant* always reminds me of the faithfulness of God. It also reminds me that I should strive to be more faithful to my faithful Lord every day.

COVET (KUH-vet)   *Exodus 20:17*

Matthew could almost taste it. He could almost taste that motorbike. He didn't care if it cost a ton of money. He didn't care if it was against the law to ride that bike on the streets and sidewalks. He didn't care that he was too young for a license. He wanted that motorbike.

Matthew talked about that bike all the time with the other guys. He drew pictures of it on his papers at school. No matter where the conversation started, Matthew always ended up talking about that motorbike. He even dreamt about it at night. Nothing else was as important or as desirable or as pleasant to consider as that little red wonder!

There is a word for Matthew's kind of desperate hungering, particularly if I (or you) wanted something so bad that you're willing to do almost anything to get it. The word is *covet*.

Have you ever coveted? It doesn't have to be a motorbike. Coveting can be directed at almost anything. Clothes. Honor. Football. Food. Special friends. Whenever you have a desire so intense that most others and other things are unimportant, that is coveting.

There are a lot of people in the world who try to make you covet. Really. The purpose of most TV commercials is to make you instantly want what they sell. Think a moment of the things you want right now. How many of them were first brought to your mind through commercials or ads? To help you see how newspaper and magazine ads stir you to covet, page through your favorite paper or magazine. Write the word *covet* on all ads that make you dissatisfied with what you have or make you hunger for things they offer. Go through one entire newspaper or magazine. Count the ads you marked. Put the number here:

_____ .

Jesus had some very pointed words for all who are struggling with covetousness. You can read them in Matthew 6:19–20. The best way to beat coveting is to walk closer to Christ.

CREATE (cree-ATE)   *Genesis 1:1*

There was a time when everything was mixed up. There was no order. There was no light. Things bubbled, exploded, froze, or simmered. That's the only way I can describe what the Bible means when it describes the world at the moment of creation as "without form and void" (Genesis 1:2). That sounds mixed up—doesn't it?

But God wasn't confused. He had a plan. He intended to bring order. He already knew how things would be. In the 38th and 39th chapters of Job, God tells what He did.

He says that He determined the seasons, and He chose the colors of creation. He put in motion wave action and star locations. He called up weather patterns with their highs and lows. He gave horses their size, strength, and beauty. He did everything. He did it without consulting even one other person. The word we use to describe all these "doings" of God is *create*.

Create means to make something orderly out of a disorderly nothing. We believe God did that. He created the whole universe and everything in it. We believe He took the nothing that was there and made it into something that now is. God created.

When we think about God and His creating, we also need to think about an important twin to "create." Without the twin, we'd be in trouble. Lutheran Christians learn to confess, "I believe God has made me and all creatures, that He has given me my body and soul, eyes, ears, and all my members, my reason and all my senses, *and still preserves them.*" God not only creates. God *preserves*. That means He continues to take care of what He made. Isn't that a wonderful partner word for create?

How about composing a prayer that thanks God for creating and preserving the whole world? Include yourself in that prayer and others. If you have the ability, why not try writing a prayer-poem? That would be nice. See if you can.

CREATOR (cree-ATE-tor)   *Isaiah 40:27–31*

The word *create* means to make out of nothing. Christians believe God took nothingness and made out of it an orderly world. For that reason, one of the names we give our God who creates is the name *Creator*.

Christians have many things to say about their Creator. The first lines of the Apostles' Creed help us to know some important things about Him. I'll start the line; you finish it. Write the next six words. "I believe in God the Father _____ ,

_____ ___ _____ _____ _____ ."

if your next words were " . . . Almighty, Maker of heaven and earth," you are absolutely correct.

We've already talked about the word *almighty*. It means just what is sounds like it means. Almighty is someone or something that has all might. But what about the other two words that describe our Creator? I mean the words *God* and *Father*.

We're going to take a closer look at each of those words in another part of this book. Right now, just think of all the describing words in the first line of the Apostles' Creed as if they were beads on a necklace. I list four: God/Father/Almighty/Maker.

Those four words say very important things about the One who loves and who created our beautiful world. They help us understand the deeper meaning of *Creator.*

First of all, those words say that the Creator is *God.* He has a proper claim to first place in our life.

Then those words state that our Creator God is like a Father to us. He gives us life and cares for us as any good daddy would. You can talk to Him.

The third thing it says is that our Creator God is Almighty. Nothing is greater than He is.

And the fourth thing that it says about our Almighty Creator God and Father is that He is the very One that made the world. He put it all together. For Himself. For us.

Those four words tell us a lot about our Creator. According to those words, He is (a) first, (b) tender, (c) strong, and (d) a doer. What a wonderful God! What a powerful Creator!

Well—what should children do with this information about the Creator? There's a very special verse in Scripture that tells us exactly what children (and other people) should do. Look at Ecclesiastes 12:1. In one word, it tells you to _____ .

CREED   *Mark 9:24*

Don't look for the word *creed* in the Bible. It's not there. While the specific word is not there, the meaning of the word surely is. Creed means "I believe." A creed is a statement of what you believe.

Most Christians use the word *creed* in connection with three great statements of belief that the church prepared many years ago: The Apostles' Creed, the Nicene (Neye-SEEN) Creed, and the Athanasian (Ath-uh-Nay-zee-un) Creed. These three great statements of faith and belief have been used by the church for more than a thousand years. They have been passed on from generation to generation. See if you can find copies of those three creeds. A good place to look is in a hymnbook.

Not only are there those three creeds—but your very life becomes a statement of what you believe. Look at these true and false statements. See how you feel about them.

1. T F When I use language which I know shames God and upsets most nice people, my creed is that I believe language like that is okay
2. T F When I do anything just so I can win a game; when I argue about every decision; when I'm even prepared to cheat to come out on top, my creed is that I must win—no matter what.

Those were easy. Try these:

3. T F When I pray in public, my creed is that I believe that God and prayer are important.
4. T F I can show how much I honor my parents by how much I do for them and how I do it.

You could actually write a creed based on the things you do. As a matter of fact, that's exactly what takes place. You are a walking *creed*.

One of the nice things is that if you look at the creed-called-you and decide you don't like what you see, you can change it. Isn't that nice? Is there anything in the creed-called-you that you would like to rewrite right now? Go ahead, erase and rewrite.

CROSS   *Galatians 6:14*

I have a collection of crosses. Many of them hang on walls of my home and office. A few are on chains and cords so that I can wear them. My crosses come in all sizes. Some are very intricate. One or two cost a lot of money. Others are made from common things—nails and bits of cloth.

Many of my crosses have different shapes. A couple are X-like. Others are little more than a long pole with a smaller crossbar near the top. One actually looks like a T. Three are so evenly proportioned that they remind me of a plus sign. No matter. The shape of the cross is not very important. The important thing is the meaning.

A cross reminds us of Jesus and how He died: that He died on the cross. But most important is knowing that He died on the cross *for us*. The cross always emphasizes the *for us*. Isn't that exciting?

The cross has another "teaching." It makes us think of something Jesus talked about in Matthew 16:24. Look that up and read it aloud.

What does it mean that we are to take up the cross and follow Him? It refers to a different kind of cross. It refers to burdens we faithfully bear as we follow Christ.

Let me make a list of things that might be crosses. You decide if they are. (1) For some people, studying is a heavy cross. (2) For some people handling their temper is a heavy cross. (3) Being born blind or suffering a lot of sickness in life can be a cross. (4) Prettiness can be a cross. (5) It's a cross to have a large weekly allowance.

Which of those five are crosses? All of them, and many other things might be, too. Like my private collection, the crosses of people are all shaped differently.

Jesus told us what to do with our cross, no matter what it looks like. We are not to complain about our cross. Or curse it. We are not to run away from it. Whatever its form, we are to pick it up, bring it along as we follow Him.

Guess what He'll do when He looks around and sees you struggling behind Him, hauling your cross along? He'll come back and help you carry your cross.

CRUCIFIX (CROO-see-fix)   *Acts 10:37—40*
There was a time when I thought crucifix was just a fancy word for cross. That's not so. "Our pastor wears a cross," said Ann on her way home with Ray. "No, he doesn't," responded Ray, "he wears a crucifix." "A cross." "No, a crucifix!" "A cross" "A crucifix!"

All the way home, Ann and Ray argued. When they got home, they appealed to their mother to settle their squabble. But Mom didn't know whether Pastor Hinz wore a cross or a crucifix, because she wasn't sure what the difference was. But she had a helpful suggestion: "Why don't you ask Pastor Hinz?" And they did.

Before we hear Pastor Hinz's answer, let me ask you. Do you know the difference between a cross and a crucifix?

The first part of Pastor Hinz's answer to Ray and Ann didn't help either of them much. He said, "I wear both. Sometimes I wear a cross. Sometimes I wear a crucifix."

Then he explained that you tell the difference between a cross and a crucifix by carefully looking at it. If the cross is just a cross—a plain cross- with no figure of Jesus "fixed" on it, you call it a cross. But if the cross has the figure of Jesus "fixed" to it, we call it a crucifix.

Cruci comes from the Latin word for cross. And *fix* comes from a Latin word that means to be fixed or fastened. Put those two together. When something is fixed to the cross, it is called a crucifix.

But Pastor Hinz wasn't done with Ann and Ray. He said, "Now I have a question for you. Do you know what a *crucifer* is?"

Ann and Ray thought and thought and thought. Finally, Ann asked, "does the *cruci* in crucifer still mean cross?"

"That's right," said the Pastor, "and the *fer* means to carry. Someone who carries a cross or a crucifix in a religious procession is called a crucifer."

Now I have some news! In one sense we are all crucifers. If you don't quite understand what I mean, look again at our devotion on the word *cross.*

DAMN
Mark 16:16

Here's one of those homonyms again. While it's pronounced the same, there are two spellings: *dam* or *damn.* A dam is a mass of concrete, or a pile of rock, or a mound of dirt that holds back a lot of water. You dam water. But the other damn is very different.

Christians believe that there are people who are damned. That means they are condemned. Damned sinners are separated from God. Forever. They spend eternity in hell. Damned people are under the wrath and punishment of God. That's what damned means. When you are damned, you are as far away from God as you can get.

It's important to understand this about the word *damn:* people are only damned by their own choice. God does not pick out some to damn and some to bless. At the Last Day, our God will announce who has refused to accept His love and forgiveness and insisted on going his or her own way, without Jesus. They are damned. But they are damned by their own choice.

Damned people are damned by what they do (sin) and what they refuse to do (believe and follow Jesus). They remind me of people who ride over the Niagara Falls in a barrel.

You know about the Niagara Falls, don't you? It's big. It's beautiful. It's dangerous. Every few years someone tries to ride over the Niagara Falls in a barrel. A very few have tried and made it in specially made barrels. But most who have tried have either been crushed by the drop onto the rocks or have drowned in the whirlpool at the base of the falls.

Those who died in that way did so of their own choosing. There are signs that say don't try to float over the falls. The advice of the police is that you shouldn't do it. The park rangers explain it's against the law and should never be attempted. But still people go ahead anyway. They disobey the law, good advice, and common sense. Their refusal destroys them.

That's the way it is with damn. God doesn't want anyone to be damned. Read John 3:16–18. To know more of the heart of the Lord also read 1 Timothy 2:4.

So why doesn't God force people to believe? Then no one would ever be damned. God wants us to be free people. Free people have choices. He helps us with our choices. He sends us His Holy Spirit so that we are led to obey. Those who refuse to hear the voice of God disobey. Only those who disobey are damned.

Pray God for strength to walk close to Him always. If you are at His side, you will never need to worry about this frightening word. Be sure you share the Good News of what Jesus wants for all people. Let your voice help others live eternally.

DEATH   *1 Corinthians 15:26*
One time, many years ago. I wrote a devotion for little children on the subject of death. The editor of the magazine for which I wrote returned my devotion. He said there was nothing wrong with what I wrote; but, he said, "Children are not interested in death."

What nonsense! Children (and other people) are as fascinated with dying as they are with being born. Children understand the truth: death and birth are twin experiences.

They are like two sides of the same coin. They are like the front and back doors of a house. Birth is one side of the coin (or the front door into life), and death is the other side of the coin (or the rear door out of life). Christians know that our Lord is standing beside both doors. As we enter life, He blesses us. As we leave life and come to Him, He welcomes us.

Without a Savior, death is a frightening thing. But Christ made the trip out the back door *and back in,* reporting to us what it was like. That's why Easter is so special. Easter is the day we remember that Christ went out the back door through death and came back in, not only proving that it's possible, but that He is stronger than death. Human death is no longer final. It does not separate us permanently.

One of the loveliest descriptions of Christian death is "the final healing." From the moment of death, there's no more pain, no more suffering, no more sickness, no more loneliness, no more hurt. All of that is over for those who fall asleep in Jesus. Christ gathers those who walk through death's door trusting in Him and keeps them as His own! He's gathering His own right now.

But death causes sadness. When someone I love dies, I am sad. Why shouldn't I be? I'm on this side of that back door. They are on the other. I cry. But I do not cry as if I have no hope. I have hope. I cry because I must wait to see them alive again. I cry as I remember all the beautiful things my friend has done for me.

I will see my friends again.

That's the exciting thing to learn from 1 Corinthians 15:19–26. Read it aloud and listen to what St. Paul says. Listen very carefully. Listen. Listen.

DENOMINATION (dee-nom-in-NAY-shun)*1 Corinthians 3:4-6*
Denomination is a word you aren't going to find in the Bible. There were no denominations in the early days of the Christian church. At least they weren't known as such. But, in Scripture, we have the sad hint of what was to come.

The simplest definition of denomination is this: it is a separate religious group with its own name (like Lutheran, Roman Catholic, Baptist) and rules. Can you think of others?

In one sense, every denomination is a sign of failure. Denominations arise when people can't work together, or when opposite beliefs develop, or when pride sticks its nose in the church, or when truths have been abused.

People in the different denominations usually believe they are right and others are wrong. Some people who take denominations very seriously argue a lot and fuss with each other. They don't always know how to be helpful toward those who they think are wrong. They divide.

Denominations must make God very sad. His plan for His people was not a hundred or a thousand fighting units battling each other! His plan was one church confronting Satan.

What can be done about these separations? How can we improve something that has been developing for so long?

For one thing, we can work to draw the church back together as one. We must work together with each other whenever we can on the basis of the Word and in support of the mission of the church that the Word puts before us. God will finally unite us in heaven. But we must still work toward that goal on earth. We must never simply agree to disagree, and let it go at that.

That means we must talk with each other. Different denominations should search the Scripture and study together. They should share the truth as they see it, testing it together against God's Word. They must always make sure that they are not letting little things separate and keep them from doing the will of God together. They can never throw out the truth that God has taught us in His Word. They can never want more than what God wants. They dare not settle for anything less.

One final thing is important as well. We must pray for each other that God would do His will in us. Pray that those who need to change may change. Make that your personal goal. List five denominations and pray for them one by one that they will let the Spirit lead them. Be sure you start with your own!

DEVIL (DEH-vul)   *James 4:7*

Is the devil real? You bet. Look at what the Scripture tells us about him. He confronted Jesus (Matthew 4:1–11). Was it real? He talked with God (Job 1:6–7). Was that real? He misled Judas (John 13:2). Was that real? He seeks to mislead you (1 Peter 5:8). Is that real?

But we're really not concerned with whether the devil is real or not. He is. The more important questions is whether we can overcome him. The answer? YES! Jesus did. With Jesus' power, we can resist him, too. That means we will push against him with all our might. Better yet, we shouldn't give him a chance to make our heart his home (Ephesians 4:27). We must fight him. We must fight him in a three-step struggle.

First start with what we know. Admit the devil is real. There's no surer way for Satan to win than to have people say he doesn't exist. Why fight what isn't?

Second, take him seriously. Cute costumes at Halloween and teasey little games about the devil don't take him seriously. Playing around with those things is like petting a hungry tiger or picking up an angry rattlesnake. Something's going to happen. All of it will be bad.

Third, confront him the way Jesus did (Luke 4:1–12). Resist him with the clear Word of God. When the devil tempts, say "No," and then use those passages of Scripture you have learned—just like Jesus did.

There's one more step, too. Stay close to Christ. Satan is nowhere near Him. The devil avoids Christ. Hold Christ's hand and the devil will never get you.

Make a little list of things you can do which will help you hold Christ's hand and fight Satan. One thing I do when I'm tempted is hum a hymn. Could you think of one that might be good to hum or sing? Starting there, make your own list.

DISCIPLE (dis-SIE-pull)   *Matthew 10:1*

Let's see. How many disciples of Jesus can you name? I'll give you the initials and you finish their names. We learned some of their names under the word *apostle*. Remember?

P_____, A_____, J_____, J_____, his brother. P_____, B_____, T_____, M_____.   J_____,   T_____, S_____, and J_____.

Those are the disciple names listed in Matthew 10:2–4. In other places some of the names are a little different.

We really don't know much about these 12 men. A little is told us in the Bible. There are also stories about some of them in other writings of the ancient world. But not much. Of the things we are told little can be proven.

So what? It's enough to know that there were 12 disciples of Jesus' choosing. We also know they sometimes did His work. Just like us. Sometimes.

What exactly is a disciple? What does that word mean? The simplest definition is that a disciple is a "learner." A disciple is a disciple as long as learning is taking place.

In order for there to be a learner, there must alway be a teacher. Who do you think was the teacher of the 12 disciples? You know the answer. Jesus.

Sometimes Jesus was called Rabbi. Rabbi means teacher.

The more important question right now is who teaches Christ's disciples today? If we are Christ's disciples, won't our teacher always be Christ?

Are you a disciple of Jesus? It depends. It depends on whether you are learning anything from Him. Test yourself. Put down five things you have learned from Jesus. It shouldn't be too hard to come up with five. When you've made your list, sign it. Write your name, place a comma after it, and add the word *disciple*. At the end of my list, I did it this way: Charles S. Mueller, disciple. I am Jesus' disciple. I have learned from Him and I am still learning.

DISCIPLINE (DIS-suh-plin)   *Matthew 11:28–30*

"What we need around here is more discipline!" said Mr. Weslock, teacher of the fourth grade. And then he started at it: he began disciplining the class. What do you think he did? How did he discipline the class?

The first thing he did was close the door so that the noise from the hall wouldn't filter into the classroom.

The second thing he did was move Helen and Richard to the front of the class, near his desk, where he could keep his eye on them. When they were watched, they did all right. Left alone, they always seemed to cause trouble for each other and for others.

Then he lined up all the desks so that everyone was looking the same way and everyone could both see and hear him.

Lastly, he told the class to remove everything from the top of their desk that was not related to the subject they were studying.

"Now," Mr. Weslock said, "We are ready to learn. We are getting more disciplined."

Does that surprise you? A lot of people think that discipline means to punish. To spank. To ground. It doesn't. Discipline means "make ready to learn."

Can you imagine why people think that punishing is the same as disciplining? I suppose it's because some folks don't seem to learn unless they are pushed around or forced to do things. That's certainly not the Christian way to discipline.

The Christian way to discipline is by helping a person control himself. It doesn't hurt to have a quiet room and good light. A positive attitude is a plus. Trained teachers, who prepare to guide the class, make this easier, too. All that is part of readiness-to-teach. But readiness-to-learn is something inside of you.

Now you think of some other things that will help discipline happen. Turn off the TV? . . .

DOCTRINE (DOK-trin)   *2 Timothy 3:15–17*

Doctrine is just another word for "a teaching." Let me explain.

You've learned about gravity. You know that in this world everything that goes up must come down. Everything. Once you've learned that, you've learned "the doctrine of gravity."

And you've learned about addition and subtraction. There are rules in addition and subtraction. Right? There are facts that must be learned. These rules and facts could be called "the doctrines of addition and subtraction."

In most schools, at some time during the day, the classes say the Pledge of Allegiance. The Pledge of Allegiance is actually a doctrine. It states a whole series of teaching about our nation. Let's pick out a few doctrines in just the first part.

One   is   that   we   are   a   r _ _ _ _ _ _ _ _ .
Another doctrine is that ours is a united nation. We claim that doctrine by saying we are " _ _ _ nation." How about the doctrine that we are "under God," and another doctrine that we are, as a nation, "indivisible?" Those are all doctrines, or teachings.

There is a lot of doctrine in the Christian faith. I'm going to list five doctrines of our beliefs. I will state them in the form of a creed (remember what that means?). Here goes:

1. I believe that God wants me to pray and that He will hear me.
2. I believe that I sin every day and always need forgiveness.
3. I believe that any who die trusting in Jesus will be taken to heaven.
4. I believe that studying the Word is necessary for growing in faith.
5. I believe that God created the world and still takes care of it.

All of those doctrines (teachings) stated as a creed (something I believe) are part of our Christian faith.

Now, can you do what I did? Can you state a doctrine that is a teaching in which you believe? One way to do this is to pick out something that the Bible teaches and that you believe. Then claim it for yourself by saving, "I believe that . . ."

Now you try it. Think of a teaching. State it as a creed. You will be presenting a doctrine.

EASTER   *John 6:40*

Let's see how smart you are. What holiday is on the fourth of July? _____. The 25th of December is what holiday? _____. The fourth Thursday of November—what holiday is that? _____.

I just know you answered Independence Day, Christmas, and Thanksgiving. Did you? Good. You are correct. But how about this one?

What holiday is the first Sunday after the first full moon after the vernal equinox (VUR-nul EE-qwee-noks)? (The vernal equinox is when spring begins: about March 21.) So what holiday is the one I described in the first sentence of this paragraph? Easter, of course.

The way we date Easter is determined by the formula I mentioned. Using that formula, the date of Easter can shift from as early March 22 to as late as April 25. It all depends on that full moon after the vernal equinox.

The dating of Easter isn't as important as the reason for Easter. Christians made Easter their first special day to recall two truths: (1) Jesus rose from the dead on Easter, victorious over sin, death, and the devil; (2) Because Christ rose, we shall rise, too. Those are such powerful doctrines that the Christian church recalls them every week. You know how? Every week we set aside the day on which Christ rose as our special day of worship: Sunday. There are a lot of Easter things to help us remember the truth of Easter. For instance, the Easter egg. We give eggs because just as a chick comes out of the egg, we will come out of the grave. Butterflies are Easter symbols, too. Think about how a butterfly gets to be a butterfly. Doesn't it come out of a cocoon? That butterfly, too, reminds us that we will come out of the cocoon of death and live eternally with God in His heaven.

The sweet candies we give at Easter remind us of the sweet truth of the Easter story. And the grass that we pack in our Easter baskets brings to our minds the coming of spring—and the new life—and growing things.

Easter is a great day. God made it that way. Now we must work to keep it that way in our own lives. By the way, when will Easter be next year? See if you can figure it out. Start with a calendar that shows the full moon.

ELECT (ee-LEK-T)   ***Romans 8:33***

Julie could hardly wait for Tuesday. It would be such a day! On Tuesday the teacher would announce which students were on the honor roll. Those who were elected would be brought to the front of the class, given a certificate, and have their name placed on the school bulletin board. It would stay there for a whole semester. A picture would be taken, too.

Even though it was supposed to be a surprise, Julie already knew that next Tuesday would be special. She already knew she had been elected to the honor roll. How did she know?

Well, last week when she had been quietly snuggled down in the corner of the family room reading a book, her dad came home from work. Not knowing Julie was there, he said to her mom, "I took Tuesday off. The boss said it was okay. We can both be there when Julie makes the honor roll."

Wow! What a thrill! Elected to the honor roll! The teachers had elected her to the honor roll! That means they looked at her grades, reviewed her conduct, talked about her class leadership and participation, and then, from among all the others, she was elected.

Elected means to be picked out. Elected is like chosen. We believe God has elected, picked out, chosen His people. And, just like Julie, we know that right now. We know of His great divine election in advance. On our "Tuesday" the truth about our election will be made public. That's all.

But there is something sad about being one of the elect. The sad thing is that some won't be there. God wanted everyone. He wanted everyone elected. Some refused. Some are refusing. Some said no. And there are some who don't know they belong among the elect because they haven't been told. God wants all for His honor roll. I think those who are the elect of God should spread the word about His great plan. Don't you think so? As one of God's elected people, shouldn't you tell others?

EPIPHANY (ee-PIFF-fan-nee)   *Matthew 2:1-12*

January 6. Remember that date. January 6. It's 12 days after Christmas. That day, January 6, 12 days after Christmas, has a special name. That day is called Epiphany.

What an odd name. Epiphany. What is Epiphany?

Epiphany is the day we celebrate the coming of the Wise Men to worship Jesus. Do you remember the story? Test yourself for a moment. How many things can you recall about the story of the coming of the Wise Men?

Did you remember the star? It was a star that led the Wise Men to Jerusalem and then to Bethlehem. And did you remember the specific directions that come from Scripture? Herod asked the religious leaders to give him directions for the Wise Men. They found some very important words in the Book of Micah.

Did you remember that there were at least two Wise Men? That's all we know. There might have been three or four or ten. All it says is that there were Wise *Men*. "Men" means more than one.

Did you remember the gifts? That's probably why we think

there were three. There were three gifts. There was gold. Everyone knows what that is. Myrrh (mur) was a substance from which perfumes and some medicines were made. Very special. And there was frankincense, a sweet gum that burned with a pleasant odor. Like incense today.

Did you remember that the Wise Men were not Jews? There were Gentiles like you and me. A Gentile is someone who is not a Jew. Epiphany meant that Jesus did not come only for the Jews. The Jews weren't the only ones elected or chosen. Jesus called (and calls) people from every race and nation. Jesus is the Savior of *all* people. That's why Epiphany is called the Gentile's Christmas.

The word *epiphany* actually means "to show," or "to appear." On Epiphany, we celebrate the fact that Christ appeared to all people and was shown to be the Savior of Gentiles, too.

Make the fanciest star you can. Let it be your Epiphany star.

EPISTLE (ee-PIH-sull)   *2 Corinthians 3:2*

"What are you doing?" Laurie asked Mike. "You are so quiet in there. Are you doing something I can do, too?"

"I'm writing an epistle," answered Mike with a lofty look, "I am busy writing an epistle."

"A what?" asked Laurie.

"An epistle," answered Mike. "You sound like you don't know what an epistle is. Everyone knows what an epistle is!"

Well, maybe Mike thinks everyone does, but Laurie didn't. Do you? Do you know what an epistle is? Guess. Guess again. See if you can figure it out.

If you guessed that an epistle is a letter, you are correct. An epistle is a letter, just like the one you write your grandmother. An epistle is a letter like the ones some send their favorite TV star or mail to their pen pal in Australia. An epistle is a piece of paper with writing on it that is stuffed in an envelope and mailed.

But who cares? What difference does it make whether you know what an epistle is or not. I doubt if you'll ever say, "I wrote an epistle," when actually what you did was write a letter.

Christians want to know what the word means so that they can understand what is being said when the Book of Romans is called "an epistle of St. Paul." That means the Book of Romans

is a l __ __ __ __ __ . The Book of Romans is a letter Paul wrote
to his friends in Rome and should be read that way. Most of
the other books in the New Testament are epistles. Not all. But
most. Look around in your Bible. See if you can find three epistles. Write their names here: (1) _____ (2)
_____ (3) _____

If your Bible says "A Letter by Paul" instead of "An Epistle by
Paul," it's the same thing. It has to be. An epistle is a letter and
a letter is an epistle. And, when on Sunday morning the pastor
says, "The Epistle for this Sunday is written in . . ." You know
that he is going to read some portion from one of the letters of
the Bible.

Isn't it nice that we are able to read these important letters?
They teach us so very much. Even though they weren't written
to us, they certainly are for us.

ETERNAL (ee-TURN-null)   ***Deuteronomy 33:27***
Most people would say that eternal is the same thing as everlasting—and that everlasting is the same thing as eternal. In
one sense, they'd be right. The two words *are* very similar.
But there is more than a hint of difference between them. Let's
see if we can find it.

Imagine with me. Imagine you are on a time journey in your
supersonic space rocket. Imagine you are zipping down a long
long road. The name of the road is *Time*.

Suppose you decide you want to start down that road in the
direction marked "To the Beginning of Time." Off you go in
your space rocket, zooming away at the speed of light. Every
hour or so, you see another sign that says, "More." Then another. And another. And yet another. Suppose you whizzed
along that way for 25 years. After 25 years, you decide you'll
never get to the beginning of time. So, you turn around. You
decide that you will go the other way toward the signs that say,
"To the End of Time." And off again, you go in that direction.

It will take 25 years just to get back to where you started.
From then on, you flash in the new direction at super speed.
And you discover the same thing. There are all those "more"
signs. Twenty-five years later, you come to a conclusion: you
can't get to the beginning of time, or the end. There is always

more. That's what eternal means. It means without a beginning and without an end.

The word *eternal* properly belongs only to God and to His will for us. He has an eternal will for us. Read John 10:10 and fill out this statement: "God's will for me is that I have ＿＿＿＿＿
＿＿＿＿＿ ."

Did you get the answer? That same hope for us is repeated dozens of times in Scripture. Our God wants us to have eternal life.

When we use the word *eternal* about people, it's different than when we use that word about God. You see, God had no beginning and no end. We are different. We have a beginning. But, in His mercy, we will have no end. Just think: heaven for us will be eternal. No end!

EVERLASTING   *John 5:24*

Mom was angry. Really angry. Jim and Carolyn knew it. They also knew why she was so upset.

All day long they had been traveling down Interstate 90 on the way to meeting their father. And all day long Jim and Carolyn had been at each other.

"Mom, Jim's pushing on my side." "Mom, Carolyn won't let me look out her window." "Mom, Jim took all the good cookies." "Mom, Carolyn marked my book." Mile after mile and hour after hour, they fussed and fought and fidgeted, until Mom just exploded.

"I've had enough of both of you. Your everlasting picking at one another has got to stop! If you don't stop, I will. I'll stop this car and you'll both get a spanking you'll never forget. Now stop it!"

Mom didn't talk that way often. But that long day with its backseat bickering and the concentration needed to drive wore her down. That's why she exploded.

Jim and Carolyn settled down. So did Mom. Arriving in Jacksonville, they got into their motel room, changed to a swimming suit and took a dip in the pool. That changed everything. Carolyn and Jim were having fun. They weren't "everlastingly picking at each other."

Remember eternal? Eternal means no beginning and no end. If you have something that doesn't have a beginning and won't have an end, it can be called eternal. Everlasting is a little different. It is more concerned with interruptions. If something keeps going *without interruption* it is everlasting. It keeps going on and on and on and on.

Close your eyes. Think about God. First think about God as being eternal. That would mean He has no beginning and no end. Then think about God as everlasting. That would mean He continuously loves us, without stopping. His everlasting love and everlasting care and everlasting concern fills all the spaces in our life. Because He is an everlasting God, there will never be even a moment when He is not deeply committed to us.

FAITH   *Romans 1:17*

Faith is like believe. Almost. But faith is a noun. It is the subject. It is a thing. Believe is a verb. It is an action word.

Let me show you how faith and believe work. If you believe an airplane can fly, that all that metal will actually get off the ground and climb into the sky, if you *believe* that, you will have *faith* in the airplane, and you will climb on board without worrying. See the difference between faith and believe?

If you believe that a doctor can put you to sleep, take out your tonsils, wake you up and fix you up good as new; if you *believe* that all that will take place, you will have *faith* in modern medicine and will prove it by planning to go to the movies two weeks after your surgery is to take place. See the difference between faith and believe? If you believe that Jesus died on the cross for your sins and that, trusting in Him, you will be forgiven and given eternal life, then you have faith in Christ and will live your days preparing to spend eternity in heaven.

Faith is the Christian's confidence. Faith is an unswerving belief. Faith claims. Faith trusts. Faith expects.

If you don't have faith in airplanes, you stay away from them.

And if you are forced to fly you develop a bad case of sweaty palms.

If you don't have faith in your doctor, you won't let him operate. If you are forced to go through surgery anyway, the hours leading to entering the hospital will be frightening.

If you don't have faith in Christ, you will reject the Holy Spirit's gift of trust and confidence in the Savior and you will go through your life hoping that you can work something out by the time you must finally face God. When we accept everything God has done for us, that is faith.

Do you have faith? There is one good way to tell. You have faith if you accept that what God has said and done is true. Nobody knows that about you except you.

FATHER   *Matthew 7:11*

Which is the better word—father or mother? That's an impossible choice.

When I was in the third grade, the girls said they liked mother best, and the boys said they like father best. But I think they were really just saying they like being what they are best.

There's nothing wrong with the question, or in trying to answer it, unless you take the answer too seriously. At different times in our lives most of us think that father is better and, other times, we think that mother is better. It depends on our needs. Each has different duties. Each has different responsibilities. But both father and mother have much in common. Both provide. Both care. Both love. Both protect. Both help.

I hope calling God "Father" means something good for you. I hope you have a father who, by his actions, helps you see how good God the Father can be. Even if your dad lets you down sometimes, I still have great news about your other Father. The heavenly Father never lets you down. He never fails. He sees your every need.

Jesus told us a lot about the Father. He even told us how to talk to Him. He said, "When you want to talk to God, say: Our Father, who . . ." (Matthew 6:9–13).

Can you finish that conversation with our Father that Jesus recommended? Write it out. Underline the important things you are asking. Because He is the good Father, He will not only hear your requests but will answer them.

FEAR   *1 Peter 2:17*

Fear is difficult to appreciate. Most people think it's bad. But sometimes it's good. Fear has many faces.

When fear means to be anxious and upset inside, it's bad. Weird noises at night fill me with fear. You, too? I don't like those noises. I don't like the nameless nervousness that comes with them.

Sometimes fear means *awe* or *respect.* I fear guns and power saws and trains racing down the track. If I didn't fear them, I could get hurt. I call that kind of fear good. It makes me careful.

Sometimes fear is little more than an inner uneasiness. Have you ever waited for your folks to pick you up after a Scout meeting or a school gathering, wondering whether they might have forgotten you? As a dad, I get nervous when the kids are late. Kids get nervous when dads are late, too. We both fear then. Is that good or bad?

All those meanings of fear fit what fear means to a Christian. In our dangerous world, there are frightening experiences with the possibility of hurt built into them. God told Abraham that there were things that would frighten him. He added, "Fear not, Abram, I am your Shield" (Genesis 15:1). With God as his shield, nothing would hurt Abraham. That's exactly how his life worked out.

But there is one other totally different sense of fear that we need to understand. We should fear God. Martin Luther explained the First Commandment by saying, "We should fear, love, and trust in God above all things." That sounds like a contradiction. Why should we fear God?

We should fear sinning against God, for unconfessed sins condemn. We should fear His wrath and the eternal separation that results from unforgiven mistakes.

But fear's not the only thing we think about. When we talk about the fear of God, we want to immediately add, with Martin Luther, that we should love and trust God, too. When love and trust come on the scene, fear fades into the background. In loving Him, we learn more of His love. Trusting Him, we know He will never hurt us.

The fear of God is only worrisome when we do not love and trust Him. Those who will neither love nor trust God are left with only one possibility: fear.

Not me. I want to walk with Jesus. I love and trust God. That takes care of fear, whether it be fear of God, or anything else.

FELLOWSHIP (FELo-ship)   *Philippians 1:5*
The Bible says it is possible to have fellowship with good things. You can also have fellowship with bad. There's such a thing as a "fellowship in the Gospel" (KJV). But there's also a "fellowship with the . . . works of darkness" (Ephesians 5:11 KJV). Look at those two. Which is good and which is bad? Fellowship means you are good, and close, friends with something or someone.

Fellowship is important. The reason it is so important is that we tend to become like the things with which we have fellowship. Let me show you what I mean.

Have you ever noticed that you argue more and hit more when you are around certain people? I wonder why. Is it because they hit and argue?

Have you ever noticed that Sunday school and church are more fun when you sit with people who enjoy Sunday school and church? And isn't it true that when you sit with those who fidget and fool around, you become a fidgeter and someone who fools around, too?

Have you noticed that it's easier to have fun when you are with others who are having fun? And that games are better when everyone is excited about what they are doing? And have you ever noticed how it can stop being fun when someone says out loud "Bor-r-r-ring!"

All those examples are illustrations of what fellowship means. Fellowship means to be close to others and to treat them as equals. That's why you become like the thing with which you have fellowship. You act like the friends with which you have fellowship. You act like the friends whom you befriend. You make them your equal—or become theirs.

Psalm 51 is about a man who wants to have fellowship with God. He asks for this fellowship in verses 10–12. Then (isn't that great?) He says He wants to go among sinners in order to be a positive influence on them. He wants to lead them back to fellowship with God. What a blessing *that* kind of fellowship is!

By the way, have you ever changed anybody or helped anybody change by being a good example? Think about the way you could do that. Think about how you can help someone by letting them have fellowship with you.

FORGIVE *Psalm 78:37–39*

"What am I going to do?" asked Lori's mom. "Whatever am I going to do?"

I wouldn't know what to do either. Lori's birthday cake was splattered all over the table. It was a mess. It had slipped out of her mom's hands and dropped. The fall was only a foot or so, but that was far enough. The layers were separated. The top part was broken in half. It looked awful. What could she do? Do you have any suggestions?

Well, no matter what you suggest, Lori's mother had an idea. She took those broken pieces and tucked them all together. Then she whipped up a batch of Lori's favorite chocolate frosting and covered the whole thing with a heavy layer of gooey delight. When she was done, you couldn't tell it had been dropped unless you looked closely. Lori's mom would know. She would know she dropped the cake, but most of us never would.

One of the nice things God does about our sins is match Lori's mom. When we ask for help with sin, and honestly confess our mistakes, He takes the broken pieces of our life, sticks them together and covers them over. He covers them over with His grace, mercy, and forgiveness. By the time He's done reworking our lives, it's almost as if nothing had happened. He covers our sins. We know there are broken parts in there, but they are now all right through God's forgiveness.

Of course, with God, covering meant a lot more than whipping up a batch of special chocolate frosting. His covering over was done through life and death of Jesus. That great sacrifice made for us covers our many faults. It covers the faults of any who ask for it.

We'll talk about the faults (God calls them sin) and the price that Christ paid later in this book. Right now, we need to understand that one of the meanings of *forgive* is "cover over." Isn't it great that God does that?

Before we go to the next two meanings of forgive, pause for a moment and look around your room. Can you see anything that has been "covered over"? Is there a slipcovered chair? A table with a tablecloth. A painted wall that used to be marked?

Look around. Find one thing. Go to it. Touch it and say, "Forgive means to cover over—just like you are." It may sound silly, but doing that will help you remember one of the greatest meanings of the word *forgive:* cover over.

FORGIVE   *1 John 1:9*

As you get older, you hear a lot of expressions. Most are self-explanatory. You know that when someone is "higher than a kite," that means they are very excited. Or if you're told something happened "faster than a speeding bullet," it took place super quick. Now one more. Have you ever heard that people who are involved in dangerous and difficult things are said "to have a tiger by the tail"? What might that mean?

Suppose you did have a tiger by the tail? What would you do? If you hung on, you would certainly be bounced around a good bit. Maybe—just maybe—that tiger would curl around and nip you off the tip of his tail, or nip you on the tip of your tail. Maybe.

The best thing would be to let go and run as fast as you could to safety. If you could let go and get out of there, you might be saved. Hanging on is not a very good solution.

What does that have to do with forgiveness? This: one of the meanings of the word *forgive* is "let go." Through forgiveness, you can "let go" of your sin and find hope and new life in Jesus Christ. He will turn your attention away from the tiger of temptation and remove the punishment that you worked so hard to deserve. He will help you reach safety in His forgiveness.

There's another way to understand the "let go" of forgiveness. You can forgive someone else. That means you can "let go" of their mistake. You don't have to hang on to their old mistakes and keep reminding yourself and them of their flaws. You can let their mistake go.

Do you want to do something that is fun? Find some balloons. Three or four. Fill them with gas that will make them rise. Helium? Take a little piece of paper and write on it just one word that makes you remember something bad you have done, or that someone else has done to you. Put your initial on it. Add the initials, J. C., for Jesus Christ. Tie that little piece of paper to the balloon. Go outside. Let it go. Good-bye! Forever. Good-bye!

Forgive means to *cover over.* It also means *let go.*

FORGIVE   *Jeremiah 31:34*

It was hard to believe. Bill read the ad three times just to make sure he understood what it was saying. The ad read: "Send your damaged digital watch to Watches Unlimited, together with $5.00 in check or money order. We will either repair or replace your digital watch and return it to you within 30 days." What a deal!

Just that morning, Bill had slammed his arm against the locker at school. He hurt his arm. But he smashed his watch. Now, for $5.00, it would be fixed.

Bill wrapped the watch just as the instructions stated. He addressed the envelope to Watches Unlimited. He made sure the $5.00 money order was inside. He sent the watch away.

One week passed. Another week passed. Another week passed. On Wednesday of the fourth week, a package was waiting for him when he got home. It was from Watches Unlimited. Inside he found his beautiful digital watch blinking away with the exact time showing. He had sent away a damaged and broken watch and had gotten back a repaired and working one. It was just as the ad had promised.

Does that sound far-fetched? It's not. There are ads that promise to repair things when you send them away. And God promises to forgive sins when we send them away. That's one of the meanings of the word *forgive.* When we send our sin to God for forgiveness, He doesn't send them back to us the same way as we brought them to Him. He takes them into His care. He cleans them up. He reshapes them and ships them back to us in a box of love, a basket of mercy, a package of new life— forgiven through Christ. How about that? When we send our sins away to Jesus, He forgives them. Sending them away while believing in Him is the same as having them forgiven.

There are three different uses of the word *forgive* in Scripture. Remember them? Make an X before all the meanings that are correct:

_____ 1. Forgive means to cover over.
_____ 2. Forgive means to forget.
_____ 3. Forgive means to send away.
_____ 4. Forgive means to pay back.

_____ 5. Forgive means to let go.
_____ 6. Forgive means to ignore.

Did you check 1, 3, and 5? Those are the correct answers. Isn't that great?

GLORY   *Matthew 16:27*

What's the brightest thing you can think of? I think the sun is the brightest thing I can think of. It's so bright you can't (and you shouldn't try) to look directly at it. The word *glory* means what the sun looks like: bright, intense, radiant.

People who make steel have a little hole in the gigantic hot furnace in which the metal melts. They peek through that hole to see whether the metal is ready yet. When they look in that hole the brightness of the fire and the molten metal is so great that they shield their faces and eyes with masks or special glasses. They call the little hole they look through "the glory hole." The brightness and the intensity of the fire reminds them of glory.

A blazing noonday sun and the intense brightness of this special hole in the furnace can suggest a beginning understanding of what glory means. A beginning.

But glory is more than just brightness. It can deal with another kind of shining quality, like "the brightness of fame" that surrounds an astronaut; the "brightness of honor" that makes us nervous when meeting the president of the United States; the "brightness of admiration" in which we hold the best student of the class. All of those "brightnesses" hint at additional parts of what glory means. Glory means awe and highest regard.

When we see something that has glory, or that is glorious, we view it as magnificent. Splendid. We are stirred to worship and praise. All that happened in the Christmas story when, according to Luke 2:9, "the glory of the Lord shone around them."

GOD

Look at the Christmas story in Luke 2 again. Add up the wonderful things that took place when the shepherds experienced the glory of the Lord. A lot happened.

GOD   *Genesis 1:1*

When it all began, this earth was a great big mixed up mess. Everything was stirred together. Nothing made sense. Then God came upon the scene with His creative force.

By His loving power, God took an intense interest in the waste and void, touched our universe, and made a world. In a moment, by His word, He set in motion all the forces that make life today lovely and complete. When He was done with what He wanted to do, He reviewed everything and gave it His stamp of approval. He said, "It is good."

What do you think good means? I think one definition of good is that it is God at work. God is good. Let me show you what I mean.

Make a series of dashes to represent four letters, like this: __ __ __ __ . Now, put a zero above the second dash so it will look like this: __ O __ __ . That's the way things were in our world before God moved in. There was a nothing. It made no sense. Everything was a zero.

Now comes the fun part. On the other three dashes, put the letters for God: G-O-D. In that order. See what happens. The meaningless zero, surrounded by God, spells G-O-O-D.

That's the way it is in many of the great moments of life. They can look like a nothing. Some even appear dangerous and evil. Then God comes onto the scene. What a change! Then nothing becomes something. The zero becomes good.

When there are difficulties at school (a zero) or at home (a zero), call upon God. When you are afraid (a zero) or concerned (a zero) call upon God. When you are nervous (a zero), seek out God and ask Him to be with you. You can do that. He says you can. Read Psalm 91:15 and see if that isn't true.

More than that, He will be with us. One of the great names of God in Scripture is Immanuel. (Sometimes it is spelled Emmanuel.) The *Im* in the name means "with." The *manu* means "us." The *el* means God. Put them all together. Start with the *el* _____, then add the *im* _____, and finally include the *manu* _____. Immanuel means: _____.

That Immanuel is our God, who can take great lumps of nothing and make good out of them. He does it every day.

GOOD FRIDAY   *Matthew 27:27–31*

You know what Good Firday is, don't you? It was the day on which Jesus died. Christians are saddened by what happened to Jesus on that Friday long ago. He was crucified, a cruel way to die.

As vengeful and evil as were the things people did to our Savior on that first Good Friday, the emphasis of our sentence should be, "Christians are saddened by what happened to *Jesus.*" In that sentence, the accent is not on *what happened,* but on *whom* it happened to.

But there is another accent that we can give that sentence. We add a few words. "Christians are saddened by what happened to Jesus *when He went to the cross because of us.*" Now that sentence states the cause of the crucifixion.

You know He died because we sinned. It's not just that some of us sinned. All of us have. Read Romans 3:23. And, while you're at it, read Ezekiel 18:4 to understand what happens to people who sin without a Savior.

But even though men were cruel to Jesus, and even though Christ died on the cross, God brought "good" out of it all: on that cruel cross where Jesus was sacrificed for all sins of all people, forgiveness was earned. Remember what forgiveness means. That's important.

I don't know why God chose to make things right between people and Himself through the sacrifice of Christ on the cross. That's a mystery too big for me—or anyone else. But I do know that, because of what happened to Jesus on that Friday so long ago, all problems between God and man are settled. At least that's true from God's side for those who will accept His gift. I am now His friend. By His power, I can now settle differences between myself and all others. It all happened because of that day.

Maybe that's why it's called Good Friday. Without those kind of good things happening, I'd have to call it Bad Friday or Frightening Friday or Wrong Friday. But in the hands of God, even that terrible day brought good. It brought me home. You, too?

GOSPEL   *Romans 1:16*

Do you know how to spell *gospel?* This is going to surprise you. You spell it e-u-a-n-ge-l-i-o-n. That's how you spell it in Greek, the original language of the New Testament. And you pronounce it ay-oo-ang-GAY-lee-on.

When the early Christians were looking around for a word tag to hook to the story of God's loving redemption of all mankind through Jesus Christ, they called it the ay-oo-ang-GEY-lee-on. What that actually means is good news. The *eu* means good. The *angelion* means message or news.

Many years later, when the people who gave us English (we call them Anglo-Saxons) wanted to find an English word for euangelion, they picked out two Anglo-Saxon words that meant the same thing: good news. One was *god*, which meant "good" in their language, and the other one was *spel*, which meant "word," or "message." It was the *godspel*. In time the letter d was dropped (it's hard to say "godspel"), and we ended up with our word, *gospel*. Gospel means good news.

No matter what the language of God's loving care for us is, it's good news. One Bible verse that says the good news clearly and with exciting simplicity is John 3:16. Look it up. Decide to do something with those words. Could you write those words with pictures and photographs? Try. Do you know how to make a collage of photos—or could you draw the letters in a special way and then color them? Think of a way to make John 3:16 look as beautiful as it sounds.

And one more thing. The word *gospel* is also used to describe the four books of the Bible in which most of the stories of Jesus' life (over 99%) are found. When it is used for that, the word is capitalized: Gospel. Those books are Matthew, Mark, Luke, and John. Together with about one percent in the Book of Acts, these four gospels tell the story, the Good Story, the story of good news in Jesus Christ. You will find the words and actions of Christ in those books. That's why they are called gospels: Good News.

GRACE   *Ephesians 2:8*

Ron knew it was coming. He knew that when the grades for class conduct were given, he would get the worst possible. He knew it because, for the past month, he had been really miserable in class. The teacher was always correcting him—with cause. He couldn't seem to control his actions. The other kids stayed away from him. He did foolish things. He did them all the time.

There was a reason for his behavior, but he didn't think he could talk about it. At home his mom and dad were fighting. He hated that. He loved both of them so much. All he wanted was that they get along. He was afraid they would get a divorce. He had even heard his dad use that word once.

He couldn't say anything at home. Whenever he spoke up, another fight seemed to start. So, when Ron got angry at himself, at his world, at his parents—he took it out on those at school. Now he knew that when he brought the report card home, his folks would start yelling and fighting again, blaming each other for Ron's failures.

When Mrs. Moeller gave out the report cards, she asked Ron to stay for a moment after class. As he waited to speak with her, he peeked at the grades which he had gotten. He was stunned. For conduct, he got a big *B*. He thought there was a mistake.

"Ron," said Mrs. Moeller, "I gave you a B for conduct. You deserve an F. You have made life miserable for everyone in this class for more than a month. I think I know why you're acting as you do. I don't excuse how you have acted. Yet as a way to show my love and concern for you, and as a way to keep you from getting in trouble at home, I have given you a B. Ron, you don't deserve it. I give it to you with love. I hope you will accept my gift and do what you can to be more like a B student in the future. But no matter, the B is yours to keep."

The B was grace. Grace means *undeserved favor*. We get grace from God. We get grace from God daily. We get it for the same reason that Ron got the B from Mrs. Moeller. Can you understand that? Can you explain that? Try it.

HALLELUJAH *Romans 19:6*

Sometimes it's spelled *hallelujah* and sometimes it's spelled *alleluia*. Both are the same word. The *hallel* means "praise" in Hebrew. The *jah* stands for Jahweh (YAH-weh), a Hebrew name that means God. Now clip those two Hebrew words together: *hallel-jah*. What does it mean? It means "praise God."

Hallelujah is angel talk. That's what angels say in heaven. We get a chance to say it here, too. It's a word of celebration. Read (or listen) to these "angel" sentences, and then respond with a hallelujah. Let's start. Say the "Hallelujah" loud.

Thank You, God, for our wonderful world/HALLELUJAH!

Thank You, God, for fun and friends/HALLELUJAH!

Thank You, God, for bicycles and roller coasters/HALLELU-JAH!

Thank You, God, for jokes and good times/HALLELUJAH!

Thank You, God, for moms and dads/HALLELUJAH!

Thank You, God, for families and love/HALLELUJAH!

Thank You, God, for pizza and ice cream/HALLELUJAH!

Thank You, God, for grace and forgiveness/HALLELUJAH!

Thank You, God, for the Bible and Baptism/HALLELUJAH!

Thank You, God, for your Spirit and Jesus Christ/HALLE-LUJAH!

Now how about thinking up some other things about which you can say "Hallelujah"?

I'd like to teach you a song. The song has only one word in the first verse. That word is hallelujah. Only you sing it "Ha-leh-loooooooooo-yah." It's like two shorter notes, a longer note, and a shorter note. Sing it that way except for the very last time you sing hallelujah. Then it's two shorter notes, and hold the last two parts of the word longer.

The notes? I'll give them to you. See if you can pick them out on a recorder, or a piano, or any other musical instrument. The word *hallelujah* is sung eight times, and the notes are these: (1) CCFF; (2) FEDD; (3) DFEE; (4) DEDC; (5) CCFF (6) FEDD;

(7) DFEE; (8) DEFF. It's an easy song to sing, and you can use other words, too. I have sung it to words like "He is risen," "How He loves me," and "I will serve Him." There are many other words that you can use. Do it. Have fun. It's the way angels have a good time. Especially, when they sing, "Hallelujah. Praise God!"

HALLOW (HAL-low)   *Matthew 6:9*

Some of the words of the prayer didn't make sense to Chuck. But he learned them anyway. He learned it the way the teacher had said. Still that one part of the Lord's Prayer sounded funny every time he said it: Hollow be Thy name? how could God's name be hollow? You mean there was nothing inside? But he said it anyway.

There came the day when Chuck's confusion about those four words of the Lord's Prayer surfaced. It happened in an interesting way.

Mrs. Black was standing at the back of the room near Chuck as the class was praying the Lord's Prayer aloud. That's when she heard him say it: "Hollow be Thy name."She didn't say anything right then. She waited.

When school was over, she took Chuck aside. She said, "It's not 'hollow be Thy name,' Chuck. It's 'hallowed be Thy name.' The word is *hallow*, not hollow." And then she explained what hallowed meant.

"Hollow wouldn't make any sense, would it?" she asked Chuck. Chuck answered that it hadn't made sense to him, but then a lot of things about religion were confusing. He didn't understand a lot of the words. Mrs. Black explained to Chuck that the word *hallow* was connected with the word holy. To hallow something means to make it holy. When it is hallowed, it is holy for you.

Now that made sense. You can only make something holy for you. After people watch you hallowing a thing, they may decide to hallow it, too. But, in the beginning, only you can hallow something—for yourself. Later, others decide whether they will hallow that thing within their own life.

But how do you hallow? I'll tell you! You show respect; you honor it; you hold it as sacred; you handle it carefully.

The Lord's Prayer asks us to hallow God's name. I'll list some ways of hallowing God's name. You decide whether they are

good ways of hallowing or not. Then you add at least one other.
1. I hallow God's name when I won't curse (Do you agree?Yes/No.)
2. I hallow God's name when I call upon Him in times of difficulty. (Do you agree? Yes/No)
3. I hallow God's name when I tell others about its power and beauty. (Do you agree? Yes/No)
    Now, you come up with a fourth. And a fifth. And a sixth.

HEAVEN (HEH-vun)   *Daniel 2:27–28a*

Let's play a game. I'll give you a word. You tell me other words that come to your mind when you hear it. Okay? Let's start: *Heaven.*

What words came to your mind? Were there five of them? If there weren't five, keep thinking. There are so many.

I came up with 10, easy. *Angel. God. Songs. Eternal. Everlasting. Praise. Fun. Crowns. Friends. Grandpas.* I came up with all of those. And then I came up with names of special people I have known, but who are now in heaven. Donnie Ewoldt; Pastor Bruening; John Krentler; Dee Hildebrandt. There are so many others. I even started thinking about Moses, Abraham, Ruth, Paul, John, Miriam, David, and Mary—all from the Bible. Will it ever be fun and exciting when we get to heaven together!

My attitude toward heaven and going to heaven is matched by that of many other Christians. But our view of heaven isn't understood by millions of other non-Christians. Some of them have never heard of Christ and the eternal life that He has made possible for those who trust in Him. Others don't believe He is getting things ready (John 14:2). Still others have never heard about the exciting gathering of saints (Revelation 21:1). There are many other things many don't know about heaven either. That's sad.

Of course, there are things about heaven I don't know. Will we wear robes in heaven? Are there puppies there? How will I recognize Mom and Dad? What about golf, baseball, fishing. swimming? I don't know about those things, but that really doesn't make much difference. What I do know is that heaven is fun and a great place to be.

The greatest fun of heaven will be seeing God and being

claimed by Him. The God whom I have loved and served here on earth is keeping a place for me in heaven. He has everything I need prepared. I know that. Heaven? Heaven is where God will take care of those who accept the eternal life that He has made possible for all (John 3:16–17).

I wonder where heaven is. Just curious! Just curious! One day I'll know.

HELL   *Luke 16:23*

Hell is the opposite of heaven. In hell, you do not see God or know He is your friend and helper. Hell is for people who do not accept what God has made possible for them. They place themselves there. Yes, I said it correctly: they place themselves in hell.

One of the great truths about life is that there are two roads you can take. One road is wide and easy to follow (Matthew 7:13). That road leads to destruction in hell. People travel down that road by ignoring what God has asked; by rejecting what God has done; by refusing to accept what God has offered. When you add all that up, it actually means that they won't take God seriously. They don't believe. The failure to believe is what puts people in hell. Let me show you what I mean.

Suppose there was a tall building and, in that building, a fire broke out. On the door of every room there are specific fire directions. Those directions show what you are to do in case of fire. There are even little diagrams. The path to safety is marked. If you follow the directions, you will escape. Now, what are you going to do? People who end up in hell ignore the diagram, the directions, the help that is offered.

There's another road mentioned in Matthew 7. It is described in verse 14. That road is narrower. It appears more difficult and demanding. Actually, it's easier to follow and a lot of fun. But it doesn't look that way. As you walk down that road, Jesus is always beside you. It's His road. He holds your hand. If it gets tough, He helps. That road leads to heaven.

I'm always sad when I think of hell. There's no need for people to go there. God doesn't want people in hell. He says so in John 3:16. The only reason people are in hell is that they refused to accept God's grace (we've had that word) and mercy (that word is coming yet). Grace and mercy are other names for the good life that can be ours in Jesus Christ. People who claim grace and mercy will never know what hell is like. Their life here on earth, and the life which is to come, will be heaven—for them. And that's what God wants for all.

HOLY   *1 Peter 3:9*

"Wait a minute, Carolyn," sputtered Grandpa. "Wait a minute! What are you doing with my wrench?"

Grandpa had come into the garage and found Carolyn whacking away at a nail with one of his best wrenches. She was hitting it just as hard as she could. At Grandpa's question, she paused for a moment, looked up innocently, and replied, "I'm just trying to bend this nail so I won't hook my coat on it."

"But that's a wrench in your hand." Grandpa said. "You don't hit nails with a wrench. If you do, the wrench will break or you will scratch the teeth or maybe even crack some of the parts. Use a hammer. Wrenches are not for hammering. They have their own special purpose. You must remember that."

I don't suppose Grandpa really knew that his explanation was almost defining the word *holy*. Holy means "set something aside for a special purpose." Things that are holy are both separate and special.

The Bible calls God holy. He is special. And He's separate—from me. Isaiah 55:8 helps me understand that! Because He is special, and separate, He doesn't act like I do. I hit back or punish. He forgives and helps. I forget and strike those who hurt me. He remembers and assists. He even gives second chances. What a wonderful holy God we have!

God also calls His children to holy lives. He wants us to live separate and special. We are to be His holy people.

Let me list a few things people like you and me might do. Put an H before those sentences that describe holy actions and an h before those that describe human action.

_____ 1. We ought to bless people who do evil things to us.

_____ 2. If we are hit first, it's okay to hit back.

_____ 3. As soon as we get to the table, we should fill our plates with the best things and start eating.

_____ 4. Don't pray before meals—ever.

_____ 5. Be alert to the needs of others and help out.

_____ 6. We should enjoy worshiping and sing songs with joy and enthusiasm.

Which of those got the H? Remember, it means "set aside for a special divine purpose." I chose 1, 5, and 6.

Now you write some sentences that express holiness. Remember what it means. Start your sentences, "Holy people will want to _____."

Can you write three of them?

HOLY SPIRIT
(Sometimes Called Holy Ghost)   *Acts 1:6–8*

The word *spirit* comes from a Latin word that means "breath," or "wind." The Greek word for spirit also means breath or wind. How appropriate! The Holy Spirit is the living breath or cooling wind in any language.

Breath cannot be seen. But breath is absolutely vital to life. It there's no breath, there's no life. That's really what the Bible tells us. When God breathed into a lump of dirt "the breath of life" and Adam became a person (Genesis 2:7), His breath brought life.

While breath or wind cannot be seen, it can be felt. You can feel a breeze against your cheek. If someone is "breathing down your neck," you know they're very close. When the Holy Spirit breathes on you, you can "feel" Him, too. You feel His presence by having faith, joy, hope, and trust.

It's not surprising that the early church described the Holy Spirit as the "breath of God." When the Spirit breathed on them, they became alive. That first great breathing took place in Acts 2:1-4. Read it. Read those words and look for ways the Spirit was felt by the people.

I noticed two things in Acts. Did you? They *felt* a rushing mighty wind. (Like the breath of God?) The disciples started acting differently. That meant others "felt" the difference.

You will spend all your Christian life learning new things about the Spirit. Start now. Start with these facts: "The Spirit is breath. He is life. He breathes life into His children. They are made alive."

And you may want to think about the ways the Spirit comes to us. The Spirit comes through the Word. The Spirit comes through Baptism. The Spirit comes in the Lord's Supper. We don't know of any other specific way. But we do know He comes through those precious "breaths."

HOSANNA (ho-ZAN-nah)   *Matthew 21:9*

Do you know what a pompon is? You've seen cheerleaders at football games and basketball games wave them. A pompon is a stick with colored paper strips attached to the end, or it can be a decorated cloth or paper ball that cheerleaders wave around.

At Jesus' time, they had something like a pompon, too. It was called a *lulab* (LOO-lab). A lulab was made of flowery branches and palm leaves tied together. During certain religious festivals, crowds would wave their lulabs and shout things like "Hosanna!" Hosanna is a Hebrew word that means "Save us, we ask." The waving and the shouting were a part of remembering that the Messiah (remember that word from when we looked at "Christ"?) was coming. They believed that when the Messiah would come, God would rule the world and save His people.

It's not surprising that people who believed Jesus was the Messiah would wave branches and shout hosanna when He came to town. As He entered Jerusalem, an excited crowd of shouters and wavers and celebrators greeted Him with lulabs and hosannas. Do you remember what they said after they shouted hosanna? Look at Matthew 21:9 and fill in the missing words: "Blessed is _____ _____ _____ in the _____ of the _____."

Many Christians still sing a hosanna. They do it when they celebrate the Lord's Supper. In the liturgy of many churches there is a song whose words are "Hosanna! Hosanna! Hosanna in the highest!" People who believe that Christ comes to them in the Lord's Supper welcome Him—just like others did a long time ago. And for the same reason. They want Him to save them.

Do you want to know something great? He granted (and grants) the hosanna wish. He saves His people from their sins.

IMMORTAL (im-MOR-tul)   *1 Corinthians 15:54*

Often when you figure out what one word means, you discover you have learned what two words mean. Immortal is one of those two-for-the-price-of-one words. If you know what immortal means, you also will know what mortal means. Mortal is the opposite of immortal. Let me show you.

Immortal is a combination word. It is a combination of *im* and *mortal*. The *im* always mean "no" or "not." An *im* turns the following word around. One of the rules of English is that when you attach an *im* to words that begin with b, m, or p, you reverse the meaning of the word. Possible with an im before it becomes impossible. Reversed! Balance becomes imbalance. Totally opposite. And mortal becomes immortal.

And *mortal? Mortal,* by itself, means "subject to death." Mortal things die. Im and mortal make immortal, which means that something won't die.

I'll list some things. You put an I before things you believe are immortal and an M before those which are mortal. Your choice will depend on whether you think they will die or not. Here we go: _____ cats; _____ fish; _____ pigeons; _____ roses; _____ parrots; _____ mountain lions; _____ earth worms.

Did you put M before all those? You should have. All those things are mortal. All will die. But there is one creature that has both an M and an I. That one creature which is mortal and becomes immortal is man. He will die, but He will not stay dead. He will not die forever. He will return to life. God has given man the kiss of immortality.

That's not good news for everyone. It could be. But some people who do not love the Lord will first die and then live forever and ever. But they will live without Jesus in hell.

Those who are led by the Spirit to accept Jesus as their Savior—who have shouted their hosannas—will live forever with Him in heaven.

Two words: mortal and immortal. Aren't you glad the second one describes you? And aren't you glad it means that you are going to spend all your eternity with Jesus in heaven?

IMPENITENT (im-PEN-ih-tent)   *Matthew 11:20*
Another one of those *im* words. When the im is hooked to most other words, it turns the meaning of the word around. That's because im means "not." Our "im" word is impenitent. The first part is im.

Now what about the other part? What about the *peni tent?* Penitent means "to be sorry or to repent." An impenitent person is someone who is not sorry.

Let me tell you a story. Keith and Richie were friends. Good friends. One day Keith did something he shouldn't have. He lied about Richie. He told his mom that the reason he didn't bring bread home was because Richie had taken the dollar she had given him. Actually, Keith had spent it for candy bars on the way to school.

Keith's mom called Richie's mom. When Richie was accused of the theft, he denied it. Nothing really came of it. It was never settled. Both moms believed their sons. But one thing did happen. After the accusation, Richie and Keith weren't friends anymore.

"Why did you do it, Keith? Why did you lie to your mom and get me in trouble?" asked Richie.

Keith never answered. Maybe he didn't know. Maybe he couldn't think of a reason. Even though both Keith and Richie knew there had been a lie, Keith never answered.

That lie didn't bother Richie as much as the fact that Keith never said he was sorry. Keith never apologized. He never really admitted he was wrong. He just glared back at Richie whenever the subject came up. He was impenitent. Totally.

And as time passed by? Richie and Keith drifted apart. At first they avoided each other. Then they just ignored one another. Their great friendship was gone. It wasn't the lie that killed the friendship. It was the impenitence.

Psalm 51 is about a man who doesn't want to be impenitent. He wants to be penitent. He asked God for help. Verse 10 outlines the road that everyone must walk if they want to move from impenitence to penitence. Look up Psalm 51, and see if you can figure out what a person needs to do in order to walk the road from impenitence to penitence.

INTERCEDE/INTERCESSOR (in-tur-SEED/in-tur-SESS-sor)
Romans 8:34

On the day that Jesus died on the cross, He was busy. He was doing a lot of things. One of the things He was doing was interceding. People who intercede are called intercessors. From the cross Jesus interceded and was our intercessor. How?

Do you remember the words He spoke from the cross? As far as we know, there were seven times that He spoke. I'll list what we know He said. You tell me when you think He was interceding.

_____ 1. Father, forgive them, they don't know what they're doing.

_____ 2. Today you will be with Me in paradise.

_____ 3. Woman, behold your son. Son, behold your mother.

_____ 4. My God, My God, why have You forsaken Me?

_____ 5. I thirst.

_____ 6. Father, into Your hands I commend My spirit.

_____ 7. It is finished.

Have your answers? I do. I think the first time and the third time He spoke were words of intercession.

The word *intercede* means "go between." A go-between helps people who are upset with each other. He calms things down by going between upset people with calming words. An intercessor makes peace and builds friendships. An intercessor tries to improve the situation. He helps renew friendships between two people who are (or might become) enemies. An intercessor helps forgiveness happen.

You have an Intercessor—an Intercessor in heaven. Christ is that Intercessor. He intercedes on our behalf between God the Father and us. He asks the Father to overlook our faults and forgive our sins. He asks the Father do to this because He has already paid their price. He asks the Father to accept His payment for our wrong and His sacrifice for our faults.

The Father does. He accepts the argument and the action of our Intercessor, Jesus Christ.

Some Go-between, this Jesus! Some Intercessor.

INTROIT (IN-troe-it)   *Psalm 100:4*

Remember the word *chancel?* Remember that "fenced in" area? And remember our worship name for the big box or table that stands in the chancel? Altar? Remember? Well, the word *introit* is connected to the chancel and to the altar. Let me explain.

The worship service begins with a confession. It's like washing our hands. And then come words of God's forgiveness for everyone. Remember what we called them? If you go back to the very first word we studied, you'll find it. The pastor faces the congregation while he says the forgiving words. While doing this, he usually stands at, or near, the center of the chancel opening, by the Communion rail.

After he speaks God's words of forgiveness to the congregation, the pastor turns and walks into the chancel and toward the altar. As he walks, or when he reaches the altar, he offers a great spiritual thought, often expressed by verses from the Psalms. From week to week the thought and verses change. Those thoughts are called the introit. The word *introit* means "to go within."

The specific verses the pastor speaks are in most hymnbooks. Look for the name of the Sunday of the church year when you are worshiping. You will find a lot of things, including the introit. The introit connects the meaning of the Epistle, the Gospel, and the Old Testament reading. It's related to the collect, too. Pick a Sunday and see if you can figure it out.

But the word *introit* not only refers to the pastor moving deeper into the chancel. When the introit is said or sung, the congregation is moving deeper into the worship service. We've washed our hands. He has rinsed them through the absolution. We're ready to enjoy God's banquet: worship.

Introit? It means enter, or go within.

INVOCATION (in-voh-KAY-shun)   *Acts 3:6*

I'll give you an invocation. "Stop *in the name of the law!*" Or how about this, "If you don't quit I'm going to get my brother! *Raymond!*"

Invoke means to call for someone or something to help you. In church we begin with an invocation, saying, "In the name of the Father, and of the Son, and of the Holy Spirit." That's an invocation. It says, "Help me do this right." You ask Him to watch you as you worship; listen as you pray; accept what you bring in your songs. The invocation calls for God's help and support in all of those things.

But the invocation also asks for the special "gifts" that the presence of God always brings. Through the invocation, we are asking for truth, faith, love, hope, and power. We ask God to come with these and other gifts. Do you realize that?

Oh, something else. Martin Luther encouraged an ancient practice on his followers. He suggested that when you invoke the name of God you make a cross on yourself. As you say "and in the name of the Son" you touch your forehead, your chest, then one shoulder followed by the other. In that way you are remembering that God, through the cross, made you His very own and gave you the right and privilege of calling upon Him. See how it works?

Don't think that this practice is strange. The cross was first put on you at your baptism. God was invoked as you began your life in His family of faith. In our earliest years our parents, the pastor, and the people of God asked Him to be with us by our baptism.

So the first thing you do in worship (and did in your faith life) is invoke God. What a great way to start. By the way, can you remember what we do at the conclusion? Can you remember what the last act of worship is called? It starts with a B. I'll give you the first letters and see if you can fill out the word. B-e-n-e _ _ _ _ _ _ _ . If you can't figure it out, go to the front of the book and see if you can't find a word that begins with the letters b-e-n-e.

JESUS   *Matthew 1:21*

Jesus. Jesus means "one who saves." Our Lord has the name of Jesus. He has that name because He is the one who saves.

Did you know that our Savior, Jesus, has more than 100 other names in the Bible. How many can you think of? I'll give you three for starters: Christ, Son of God, Savior. Now you make your list.

I have more names for your list. How about these: *Advocate* (1 John 2:1); *almighty* (we had that one—remember?); *Alpha* and *Omega* (Revelation 1:8). Alpha and Omega are the first and the last letters in the Greek alphabet. Can you think why Jesus would be called that?

In Matthew 3:17, His Father calls Jesus the *"Beloved Son,"* and in Luke 1:78, Jesus is called the *Dayspring* (KJV). Dayspring is another word for dawn. See if you can figure that name out.

The advent hymn, "Oh, Come, Oh, Come, Emmanuel" has many names for Jesus. One name is *Emmanuel* (that means "God with us"). In the rest of the verses, He is called *Wisdom from on high, Lord of might, Rod of Jesse, Key of David, Desire of nations.* All of those are titles from Scripture used to describe Jesus. And there are more.

I haven't mentioned *King of kings, Lord of lords, Lamb of God, Leader, Good Shepherd, the Way, the Truth, the Life, the Lord of glory, Redeemer, Prince of peace, Son of David, the Word,* or *the Morning Star.*

Now go back over all the names I have mentioned. Put a little mark before every name of Jesus you have heard before. Just a little checkmark. Everytime you find another name, write it on the margin of this page. Better write small! There are a lot more of them!

When you have written all the names of our Lord, there is still that one which, in my opinion, tops them all. It's the name the angel told Joseph to use for that little baby: *Jesus.* Jesus saves His people. Jesus saves you and me.

What a wonderful name! Jesus. No wonder the angel told His parents to give Him that name.

JUDGE   *Psalm 96:10-13*

It was the Montgomery County Fair, and Lee was about to be judged. Lee had baked cookies. He brought them to the 4-H section of the fair, where the cookie competition was going on. He brought them there on a dare.

His sisters had told him he didn't know how to bake. They said that even if he tried to compete his cookies wouldn't be any good.

That's all the challenge he needed. With their words of discouragement ringing in his ears, he was determined to bake cookies no matter what. He just knew they would be the best ever. He said so.

Now the bragging time was past. He was in the big hall. Table after table was covered with all kinds of delicious-looking cookies and cakes. Dozens of young bakers were waiting for the judge. The judge came.

First she looked over the whole lot. Then she started testing. She nibbled here. She looked carefully there. After an endless amount of time, she reached into her bag, pulled out a big blue ribbon and, with a flurry, stuck it into the winning plate of cookies. Guess what! Lee won! He was the blue ribbon winner. He had been judged. Judging wasn't nearly as bad an experience as he had expected!

Christians believe they will be judged. Not as cookie bakers. They will be judged as people. Christians believe God will judge every person in the world. They state that in the Apostles' Creed—and the Nicene Creed, too. Look at those creeds. Find the words in both creeds that say God will judge. Write them here: _____

_____

The nicest thing about God's judging is that Christians don't have to be nervous about it. Christians already know who the winners are. They know the Judge will say, "Come into My house, My child. You are forgiven. Jesus has paid your debt and made you part of the family." That's what the Judge will say to those who trust in all that Jesus has done.

Others will have a tougher time. Those who insist on being judged by what they've done, without Christ, will get what they ask for. God will give a judgment. It will be fair. It will be just. But those results also are already known. No blue ribbons. No heaven. No forgiveness.

It's not that He doesn't want to forgive! But if they insist on standing on their own, that's the way it will be. For them the Judge will be no friend, and the judgment will be no fun.

But not us. We believe our Judge will give us what we could never earn: life eternal. I think we ought to tell everyone of this better way of being judged.

JUSTIFY (JUS-tee-fie)   *Titus 3:4–7*

Remember those *im* words? Remember what the im did to words? If you put an im before many words that start with a B or an M or a P, their meaning is reversed. Possible becomes impossible. Reversed. Perfect turns into imperfect. Reversed. Penitent comes out as impenitent. Reversed. And there's improbable and immortal. All reversed.

Well, not only are there im words, there are also *fy* words. When a fy is attached to a word such as glori*fy* or sancti*fy* or magni*fy*, those two letters added mean "to make." Glorify means to make glorious. Sanctify means to make holy. Magnify means to make big. And justify? It means "to make just."

When something is "made just," it has been made perfect, or straight, or correct. Justifying your actions means you are explaining that you did the right thing. If you justify a friend, you are claiming his actions were proper. Justify means to make something right. *Really* right.

God justifies us. Isn't that nice? On Judgment Day, with God as our Judge, we will be justified. We won't just barely sneak into heaven by the skin of our teeth! We will walk in the front door, chin up, hand-in-hand with Jesus. All the bad things we have ever done, no matter what they are, are then and there forgiven. He covers them over. He sends them away. He lets them go. He gets rid of them. In their place, God will pile up all that Christ has done and put our name on that pile. That's how He will justify us.

He wants to, and will, do the same for all who accept His forgiveness. All of Christ's goodness and all of Christ's faithfulness and all of Christ's willingness to do the wishes of His heavenly Father will be ours, just as if we did it. Justifying covers all the wrongs each one of us has done, or ever will do.

Why does God to this? Grace. Remember that word? Undeserved favor! We are justified by grace, through faith in Jesus Christ. God makes me what I never could become by myself. He makes me pure.

As a justified child of the Father, I work hard, by His Spirit's power, to do those things which honor Him, which help others, and which bring blessings to me. All this because I am justified.

KING
Zechariah 14:9

There was a time when the greatest thing to be in all creation was king. Kings were in absolute charge. When they spoke, they were believed. When they wanted something done, it was accomplished. When they asked for anything, they got it.

I don't suppose it was ever absolutely that way. There had to be those who disagreed with the king; some people who disobeyed.

But they didn't do their disobeying very publicly. If a person was caught disagreeing with or disobeying the king, a terrible punishment took place. That's why most folks tried to look like they were listening and agreeing. But having a king meant other problems, too. One big problem was that they changed as they got older. And most times they changed for the worse. Many started out doing good and helping people. In time, they forgot their early goals and good intentions. They turned into bad kings. That was hard for the people they ruled.

In the Bible (and in history) there are a few good kings. But there are many more bad ones. It's just so hard to stay good as a king. There are so many temptations. And you begin believing your press agents.

But aren't we blessed! Our only King is a good King. He created and now rules heaven and earth. We can tell He is a good King by looking around at what He has given us to use and how well He takes care of His gifts. He gave us the sun and the seasons and sleep. He created birds and warm days and families. He thought of food and fun and beaches. He made this a technicolor world and packed it with wonderful people. What a King! And He lets me live here, too!

This King of ours cares not only for the here and now. He is concerned about our future. He wants us all to be under His rule not only in this world, but in His eternal kingdom in heaven hereafter. He has provided the way so that our enemies will not stop us from being with Him.

We sure have a good King. Don't you want to keep Him? Check the things you can do to make sure He remains a powerful and reigning Lord of your life:

_____ Build a throne for Him in your heart.

_____ Crown Him the Lord of your everyday.

_____ Obey His Word and directions.

_____ Make sure He has no competition.

Four for Four? That's what I checked! Now let's do it!

KINGDOM OF GOD   *Luke 9:62*

The Bible often speaks of the kingdom of God. It sometimes calls it the kingdom of heaven. Do you know where the Kingdom is? If you look on a map, you won't find it. The kingdom of God is not a place. It is always people. The kingdom of God is wherever God is ruling the life of His people. The Kingdom is anywhere His people are. The Kingdom is more like a condition. It's a state of mind. It's an understanding.

One way to better understand the kingdom of God is by learning about embassies. An embassy is a building, in any country, where the official representative of another country lives and does business. For example, the Unites States has embassies in Germany, England, Russia, Brazil, and almost every other nation in the world. Other countries have embassies in our country, too. Now comes the interesting part.

Every embassy, even though it is in another country, is considered a part of the country it represents. Within the boundaries of an embassy building, the laws of the country that owns it are practiced.

It's the same with the kingdom of God. Wherever God is honored as King, the kingdom of God is found. The kingdom of God is within everyone who trusts in Jesus and recognizes His ruling power. Where He is, He rules. Where He rules, He is.

We mention the kingdom of God in the Lord's Prayer. Do you remember what we say there? "Thy kingdom _____ ." That means we want it to come *to us*. We want it to be *in us*. The Kingdom comes to us and others when Christ is accepted and

His good gifts are claimed. The kingdom of God exists wherever Christ is recognized as King.

While you can't see the Kingdom, you can see signs of the Kingdom. You see them in the actions and in the attitudes of the King's people. Let me give you some examples, and you check whether they are indicators of the possible presence of the kingdom of God.

_____ Ginny wears a cross.

_____ Mark got angry and hit Ray, but afterward he was sorry and apologized.

_____ Mrs. Morris helped Marvin get up when he fell on the playground.

_____ Norma asked her mother whether she could help set the table.

_____ Kyle prays to Jesus when he is in trouble *and* when he is happy.

_____ Audrey trusts that she has a home in heaven with Jesus.

I think those are all signs of the Kingdom. What do you think? Can you suggest others?

LAMB OF GOD   *John 1:29*

People who lived before Christ had many different ways of trying to please God. One was through sacrifices. Sacrifices were special gifts brought to the Lord. They were usually burned on an altar. Sacrificing was a way of admitting wrong, asking for forgiveness, showing trust, and expressing love.

One very impressive and important sacrifice was that of a lamb. To sacrifice a lamb was to offer something very valuable. Grown up, the lamb could provide wool and meat and other sheep. A sacrificed lamb could do none of those things.

But people sacrificed lambs anyway. There were even rules about it. The lamb couldn't be a runt. No sick or injured animals were sacrificed. A healthy lamb was required. It had to be the best. That's what made this sacrifice so special. The best was brought.

Throughout the Old Testament, lambs were sacrificed. But every time one was brought, another was needed. The people sinned again and again and again. They had to bring a lamb, and another lamb, and yet another lamb. Until . . .

One day John the Baptizer saw Jesus. He understood who Jesus was and what He would do. He said, "Look! There is the *Lamb of God* that will take away the sins of the world." Up to then, the lambs were the lambs of men. Now came the one, perfect, final *Lamb of God*.

Without flaw? The best? Yes! That's Jesus. When God sends a sacrifice, there is none better. Most important, Christ is the final sacrifice. No more lambs are needed. As the sacrificed lamb, He would not only atone for some sins of some people for a little while, but God's Lamb would atone for all the sins of all people for all time.

On Communion Sundays many congregations sing a song called the Agnus Dei. That title means Lamb (Agnus) of God (Dei). Find it in the liturgy. The first line is "O Christ, the Lamb of God, . . . have mercy on us." He did. He still does.

LAW   *Romans 3:20*

The Old West was sure wild. What else could it be? There was no law. There were no marshals. No judges. No sheriffs. Any person big enough and strong enough and fast enough could do whatever he wanted. In those lawless times, many innocent people were hurt. Some were even killed. When things changed for the better in any part of the West, it always happend for the same reason: a lawman came to town.

Think of the movies and TV programs you've seen about lawmen. Texas Rangers, United States marshals. Sheriffs.

To really be effective, a lawman had to be backed by a judge, a court, and a jail. When all those things were in place the West settled down. It wasn't nearly as wild. Lawbreakers were caught by the marshal, tried by the judge, and put in the jail. Just like that. Law brought order.

We've written a lot of laws since the time of the old West. Our laws are not always good. Some are good for a few and bad for many. Some laws make sense in one place, but no sense at all in another. Sometimes we make too many laws. Sometimes laws conflict.

One of the most important things to know about laws is that, while they can help to keep people from killing each other, they can't make them love one another. The law may protect your property, but the law can't force folks to help you improve your buildings and business with their assistance and good advice. The law has definite limits. In a disorderly world, it brings the beginnings of order. But after order is established, something very different is required to make life better. Love.

It's the same with God's law. God gave laws (the Ten Commandments) to a lawless world. But the Ten Commandments don't make people better. At least, the Ten Commandments keep people from ignorantly doing obvious wrong. Or, the Law shows people how far from perfect they are. And the Law established boundaries of good conduct. But when we try to live by the Law in order to get God's favor, those laws of God turn on us and expose our faults. They do not bring peace. Life under the Law, with no love, is in many ways as bad as life with no law at all.

Christians don't live under the Law with no love. As Christians we have Christ to protect us from the Law's anger and burning force. He brings His love into our lives and shows us how to tame the pain and fright of the Law with His grace and mercy. Led by His love, the Law becomes a useful friend that shows us more clearly God's intended pattern for the good life.

LECTERN/LECTOR   *Luke 4:16*

"I'm going to be the lector next Sunday," said Amy's dad to the family.

"Lector?" asked Amy. "What's a lector?"

Amy was seven years old. She had never heard of a lector before. On TV she had heard of electrons and elections and lectures. But lector was new to her.

"You know what a lector is, Amy," answered her dad. "A lector is a fancy name for the person who reads the Bible each Sunday in our church service. Sometimes the pastor reads from that little stand. Sometimes different people in the congregation come up to the chancel and read. Those are lectors."

"Oh, yes," said Amy, "Now I know. They stand at that little desk and talk into the microphone. They don't always talk loud enough. Sometimes they stumble over words."

"You're right about that, Amy. Most people have trouble reading the Bible out loud. A lot of the words are tough to pronounce. And they're just as tough to understand. But *lector* isn't one of those Bible words that is tough to understand or pronounce. It's not a Bible word at all. Simply put, a lector is a reader. It would sure be easier to call them that."

"The stand with the light and the microphone from which they read has a name, too. It's not a Bible word, either. It's called a *lectern*. A *lector* stands at the *lectern* and reads. Can you say that with me?"

It took Amy a couple of tries to get it straight. Finally she got it out. She even understood the difference. It helped a little to remember all this when her dad explained that in many churches, the lectern is at the opposite side of the chancel from the pulpit. Is that true in your church? Why don't you draw a plan of your chancel? Make a mark where the altar is located—and the pulpit—and the lectern.

If your church doesn't have a lectern, ask your pastor about it. Some churches don't have a lectern for a reason. He'll know the answer. After he has explained it to you, you'll know the answer, too.

LENT   *Matthew 4:1–2*

Forty is a favorite Christian number. It keeps popping up in the Bible. At the time of the great flood the rain fell for 40 days. The Children of Israel wandered around the wilderness for 40 years. Jesus fasted before His temptation for 40 days. There are many other 40s in the lives of Moses and Joshua and in various events of Scripture.

The many 40s were the reason early Christians chose to set the boundaries of the season of Lent at 40 days.

Lent starts 40 days before Easter, *not counting the Sundays.* Sundays are not counted in Lent because those days are already set aside as a weekly reminder of the resurrection of Jesus. And we're reminded of our resurrection, too. So, Lent has no Sundays.

Lent is a time when Christians think about repentence. It's

a time of turning around and of changing. The color of the altar cloths is purple or violet. Those are the colors of penitence. The music is quieter and even a little sad. The sermons refer more to the special sufferings of Jesus on the cross and the price He paid to save us.

The first day of Lent is called *Ash Wednesday.* Lent reaches its peak during *Holy Week,* the week between Palm Sunday and Easter. Two days within Holy Week have special names: Maundy Thursday and Good Friday. Otherwise, the days of Holy Week are called Holy Monday, Holy Tuesday, Holy Wednesday, and Holy Saturday.

The word *Lent* actually means *spring.* North of the equator Lent always comes in the spring of the year. There the buds are forming and early flowers bloom during Lent. Those signs from nature tell us that warmer, brighter days are not far away. The beginning of Lent tells us that the spiritual summer of Easter is not far away, either.

During Lent, Christians get ready for an exciting celebration of the Resurrection. Lent is our readying time. We ready our hearts, our lives, and our thoughts. Any suggestions on how that readying might be done better in your home, in your school, and in your church? Time to talk, maybe?

LIFE   *Genesis 2:7*

What is life? If you had to decide that based on the way we use the word, any definition would be tough. We talk about the love of *life, life* of the party, country *life, life* sentence, *life* of poverty, everlasting *life.* And there are others. You've heard of "bring to life," "take a life," and "true to life."

So I ask again. What is life? Think about it and write your definition: Life is _____ .

It would be almost impossible to write a wrong definition. Whatever you answer, it at least reflects how you feel about life. You could even end the definition of life with ". . . when you are not dead." That would be true. But there is more to life than that.

Being alive—really alive—means that you are keenly aware of what's going on. People who are unconscious are living, but I don't think they really have life. After God breathed into Adam the breath of life he was alert. He was aware. He had to be. He had work to do in the Garden of Eden with God.

And when Jesus said "I [have come] that [you might] have life and have it abundantly" (John 10:10), He meant more than that we would be breathing. It surely indicates being alive to God (Romans 6:11). God makes the abundant life vigorous, active, very alert and full of the Lord's will. Because He is in the life it's fun, too!

Think for a moment about life and what it means to you. When you finish reflecting on life see what you can do with this incomplete poem:

Life is a special gift from God

That _____

_____

_____

Finish it either as a four-line rhyming verse or as a poetic statement of any kind.

LITURGY (LIT-tur-gee)   *Luke 1:5-11*

Liturgy is one of the most interesting words for something in their God-life that early Christians selected. It, too, is not a Bible word. At least it's not a Bible word in the way we use it. But the hint of our use is everywhere in Scripture—like in the reading about Zachariah. Let me tell you about the word *liturgy*.

A long time ago in Athens (that's a city in what we now call Greece), the rich people were thought to have special responsibilities. They were expected to do costly things for the other citizens of the city from time to time. The common people figured that the rich people shouldn't be the only ones to get good things. Some rich people paid for a carnival so that all the people could have fun. Some rich people hired actors to put on plays for all the other citizens. In time of war, some rich people paid for arming soldiers or preparing a ship for battle. They were expected to do those things.

All of those special expectations of service were called *leitourgia* (lie-toor-GEE-ah).

After the resurrection of Jesus, Christian people gathered each week for a service honoring God. They met on Sunday.

(Later I'll tell you why they chose Sunday.) They also met on other important Christian festivals, just like we do.

When the Christians gathered together, they had special readings and special hymns and special preaching and special prayers. Can you guess what they called all of that special service to God? They called it *leitourgia*. They figured that people who were *rich* in faith and *rich* in trust and *rich* in hope and *rich* in the Gospel could naturally be expected to share their *richness* with other people through song and witness and worship. They figured the richness of God's people was like the richness of people who had money in Greece.

Nowadays, we pronounce the word a little different. We don't say *leitourgia*. We say *liturgy*. It's almost the same word in sound. It is the same word in meaning.

Our Sunday worship service from the invocation (the beginning) to the benediction (the end) is one long and wonderful leitourgia. It is a liturgy, an expected special service to God brought by the rich. We say some liturgy. We sing some liturgy. We share the liturgy. And why not? Who's richer than we are? If the Greeks could do it because they were money-rich, we can do it because we are love-rich.

LORD   *Acts 10:36*

In some lands, people are called lords if they are powerful and if they have total control of someone's life. One place they use that term today is in England. Do you know others? I do. How about in the church? We call God Lord.

Calling God Lord is not the same thing as making sure He is the Lord of your life. Jesus said He is a person's only true Lord when—

_____ a. His followers don't forget to shine their shoes on Sunday.

_____ b. They do what He tells them to do.

_____ c. They stand as the pastor comes into the room.

_____ d. They say the Pledge of Allegiance to the flag.

Did you pick one of those? If you're not sure what the answer is, look at Luke 6:46.

Did you give the correct answer? I put a check in front of b. To be really sure whether you understand how Jesus is truly Lord, finish the following sentence with two different endings of your own choosing. The sentence begins like this: "Jesus is the Lord of my life when I—

a. _____."

b. _____."

How did you finish it? My first completion was (a) pray to Him in times of need. My second was (b) trust Him for forgiveness.

There are a lot of good endings to that sentence. The ones that I wrote were only the first that came to my mind. I'm sure if I thought longer I would come up with more. And I'm also sure that your answers are as good as mine.

We're not the only ones who talk about Jesus as Lord of our life. Hymn writers have done that for centuries. I looked in one hymnbook and found 29 hymns that begin with the word *Lord*. There's no telling how many have the word *Lord* somewhere within their verses. Can you find one? Or two? Or maybe three?

St. Thomas once said a wonderful Lord-thing about Jesus. He called Him, "My Lord, and my God" (John 20:28). Tonight consider ending your prayers this way: "I end my prayers in the name of Jesus Christ, my Lord and my God." Include in your prayers a request for faith so that you always keep Jesus as your Lord.

LOVE   *1 John 4:8*

There is no subject about which more songs have been written than love. Do you know why there are so many love songs in the world? I do.

There are so many love songs because love is nowhere defined. It's not defined in a dictionary. It's not defined in the Bible. Love is not defined. Love is only described.

Love is an action. It is a constantly changing action. There will be as many new love songs as there are new actions. And since new actions are developed every day, new descriptions will always follow, like, "Our love is like a rocket to Mars . . . or a week in Disneyland . . . or whatever."

You see, love is tied to what you do, what you can do, and what you want to do. Let me explain.

Did your dad ever say, "If you love me, you would make your bed—or take out the trash—or do your homework—or let me nap?" Some people try to turn your love into an action. If you love them, you will do something.

It was the same way with God. The only difference was He didn't ask *you* to do anything. *He* did something for you—and for all of us. Read John 3:16 and complete this sentence: "For God so loved the world _____

_____ ."

God acted. God acted out of love.

Here are a series of *love/action* sentences. I'll start them; you finish them. Finish them any way that makes sense to you.

1. When you love a friend, you will _____

_____ .

2. When you love your parents, you _____

_____ .

3. When mom and dad love you, they will _____

_____ .

4. When people love God, they _____

_____ .

5. When a pastor loves his congregation, he _____

_____ .

Love always ends up as an action. There's more than emotion in love. There's motion.

So let's get it straight and keep it straight. Love is an action.

MAGNIFICAT (mag-NIF-ee-kot)   *Luke 1:46-55*

Elizabeth was the mother of John the Baptist. She was an older woman.

Mary was the mother of Jesus Christ. She was most likely a young woman.

Mary and Elizabeth were cousins. That meant Jesus and John were relatives, too. Even though these boys were relatives, they loved each other. John said about Jesus, "Behold the Lamb of God" (John 1:29). And do you know what Jesus said about

John? "Among those born of women there has not risen anyone greater" (Matthew 11:11 NIV). They were relatives. They were good friends. They said nice things about each other.

Just before they were born (John was born a few months before Jesus), Mary came to visit Elizabeth. As soon as Mary entered the room, Elizabeth somehow knew that something special was about to happen. She said she even felt John move around inside her. Whatever made her do it, Elizabeth praised God, and praised Mary, and praised the baby Mary would have—Jesus.

Mary answered Elizabeth's words with a beautiful song honoring God. In her song, she said many great things. You can read that song in Luke 1:46–55. Do that, and then review the list of things I suggest below. Put an *M* in front of everything Mary said in her special song.

She said:

_____ God has been very good to me even though I'm not important.

_____ He has also promised to show mercy to others who fear Him.

_____ God helps people in trouble.

_____ He helps because He promises He will.

_____ I wish God would let me alone.

Where did you put your M's? The first word of Mary's prayer of praise, in Latin, is *magnificat*. *Magnificat* means what it almost sounds like. It means to magnify; make larger. That's what Mary wanted to do. She wanted to magnify her respect for the Lord. Because magnificat is the first word she spoke, the whole song is called the Magnificat.

If you want to know how that song sounds today, look in your hymnbook for the order of service which we call the vespers. The Magnificat is usually sung during the vespers. There are different tunes for those words. Find a tune you like and see if you can sing the words of the Magnificat.

MAN   *Psalm 8:4*

By now, you've guessed it. I like words. The more I know about a word, the more I know about what the word wants to teach me about life, about myself, and about others. Take the word *man*, for instance.

Guess what the word *man* is in Hebrew. Don't be surprised. You know the answer. You do. I'll give you a hint. The word *man* in Hebrew is the same as the name of the first human being. Got it? *Adam.* Adam means man.

In Greek, the word for man is *anthropos* (AN-throw-poss). In college, they teach courses in anthropology. Anthropology is the study of man. (Try that all out on your folks at supper. See who knows the Greek and Hebrew words for man.)

Man doesn't just refer to boys—to males. The word *man* is one which can be used for men and women; for boys and girls; for you and me and all other people in the world. It is a collective word that refers to all human beings.

God is "mindful" of man. His mind is full of good thoughts toward men and women. Because God is mindful of all people, He makes sure we have things. Let's make a list of the good things God gives us *because He is mindful.* I'll start with some; you add. How about families (for fun and protection); ice (for ice cream, ice skating, and ice drinks); and kangaroos (for laughter). Now you add things our mindful God has given. Five, maybe? If you are with others, take turns building a list.

By the way, have you been mindful of any man today? Have you thought with concern about another person? Why don't you do that now. Either say a prayer asking God to be with someone in need (if that's what made you think of them) or that He bless your memory pal with special love and care for the good way you feel toward him or her.

If you don't have a caring, loving thought about any man, bring that word into your mind and caress it with tenderness until you think of something. Let your mind be "full" of the meaning of "man" while you work at being mindful of just one.

And guess what?! Tomorrow you can add another to your concern list. And then another. And another. And yet another.

MATINS (MA-tins)   *Psalm 5:3*

Many, many years ago, actually a thousand or more, there were Christians who gave their entire life over to the worship of God. All their life. Every day. All the time. Those who were women were called nuns. They lived in buildings called convents (KON-vents). The men who did this were called monks. They lived in monasteries (MON-ah-stair-eez). That word, *monk*, and monastery, come from the same Latin word that really means, "I want to be alone."

These very religious people, even though alone, lived a life of strict order. They ate at special times. They worked and worshiped at special times. Their worship was so regular and ordered that their times of prayer and praise had names.

For instance, the first period of worship each day was called *matins*. Matins means "morning" or "dawn." At first, matins took place right after midnight, when a new day was beginning. In time, matins was celebrated at 6 a.m., the time when dawn takes place through much of the year.

As time went on, matins became the name given to any service that took place in the morning before nine. Now matins can take place as late as noon. (Sounds like we're getting lazier.)

Can you find the "Order of Matins" or the matins service in your hymnal? Almost every hymnal has one. Matins usually begins with the leader saying, "O Lord, open my lips." The congregation responds, "And my mouth shall show forth Your praise." Those words from Psalm 51:15 are a wonderful way to start worship at any time of the day. They are especially good for starting early morning worship.

It's good to know where matins come from. Knowing this helps us remember that there have always been people who loved the Lord and who worshiped Him with joy—even when they didn't have to.

Why don't you look up *monks, nuns, convents,* and *monasteries* in an encyclopedia? You'll be surprised by all you will learn.

MAUNDY THURSDAY (MAWN-dee)   *John 15:12*

I'm so silly. I once thought that people were saying *Monday Thursday.* That didn't make any sense. How could one day be Monday and Thursday at the same time?

But the word isn't Monday. It's *Maundy.* Maundy means "command." You could call Maundy Thursday the Command Thursday. Maundy Thursday is the Thursday in Holy Week. Holy Week is the week between Palm Sunday and Easter. On Maundy Thursday, Christ gave a special command. Let me tell you about it.

He had just finished washing the disciples' feet. That made

them uncomfortable. Peter said, "I can't let you do that to me, Lord." Jesus said, "If I don't wash your feet, you can't have anything to do with me." Peter did what Christ wanted.

When Christ had finished washing the feet of all the disciples, He said, "Now I want you to wash . . ." They thought the sentence would end with " . . . *My feet.*" He ended the sentence by saying, "one another's feet." He wanted them to lovingly serve one another. He made that desire clear by giving a command about loving service. He commanded, "Love one another."

Then, in order to further knit His disciples together as a family of faith, Jesus gave them a special uniting gift: the Lord's Supper. Maundy Thursday is the day on which the Lord's Supper was given. The washing of feet, the command to love, the Holy Eucharist—all were part of Maundy Thursday.

But what does it mean that He commanded love? Think about it for a moment. Do you remember what we learned about love earlier in the book? We learned that love is an action. This command to love is calling us to action. So let's *act.* Now!

Choose your mom, your dad, or maybe a grandparent. Figure out something you can do that will be a living of love—an action. Write your plan. Spell out how you are going to "do" love. Within the next 24 hours, or as soon as you can, carry out your decision. Answer Christ's command. And think of Maundy Thursday—and His action plans—and what He did.

MEDIATOR   *1 Timothy 2:5*

David and Brian despised each other. At least that's what they said. They fought constantly. The whole class knew something had to be done. As long as they kept at each other, there would be no peace for the rest of the class.

Sally came up with an answer. She said, "I'm sick and tired of those two going at each other all the time. Most things they fuss about are stupid. They need someone to help settle things without fighting. They need a *mediator.*"

A mediator? A mediator? They need a *mediator?*

In the business world, there are sometimes differences between workers and the company for which they work. When the differences get out of hand, there can be a strike. And if the strike lasts too long, the government appoints a mediator. His job is to help the two parties settle their differences. He does this by mediating. Let me show you how it works, using David and Brian as examples.

Draw two circles about the size of a nickel. Place them a half-inch apart. In one circle write the name David. In the other circle write the name Brian. Draw some sharp points on the facing side of both circles. Those points represent the way David and Brian are always ready to fight.

Now, draw a third circle that touches those two circles. Put it right between. Make it large enough to cover the points. In that circle, write the name Mark. You see, Mark was the one whom the class chose to be the mediator. He was as big as David and Brian. Both liked him. Whenever the two of them started to fuss and fight, Mark moved in and helped to settle the differences. Mark was the mediator. He stood in the middle. Peace came to the class.

God has a Mediator, too. He has placed *loving Jesus* (connecting circle) between *sinful us* (circle 1) and *perfect Him* (circle 2). Jesus settles the differences that develop between God and us. But He does that in a way that is different from that of Mark. Jesus doesn't just talk us into being better to God. That really wouldn't work. He takes upon Himself all the mistakes that we make; all the sins that we do; all the arguing that we start—and covers them with His love and forgiveness. Mark couldn't do that! And, on top of it all, He comes into our hearts to change our lives. He's *some* mediator!

Draw two more circles the same size as before. Put your name in one. Put God's name in the other. Add those pointy arrows. Call the arrows from our circle sin. Call the other arrows from God's circle judgment. Now draw a linking circle. Call that circle Christ. Put a cross in the middle of it. Under the cross, put some more words. Write, "The Mediator." Jesus is our Mediator. He mediates. Peace comes. Isn't that nice?

MERCY   *Jude 21*

The word *mercy* can be found in all parts of the Bible. An Old Testament example is Psalm 118:1 (KJV), "O give thanks unto the Lord, for He is good; because His mercy endureth _____ _____ ." (Find that last word.)

In the New Testament, there are many beautiful "mercy" passages. 1 Timothy 1:2 uses mercy as the link between two other great virtues. The first is g_____ . The second is mercy. The third is p_____ . Grace and mercy result in peace.

But what's the difference between grace and mercy? Are they the same thing? Well, let's see.

You already know about grace. How about checking it again. Remember that grace is "getting what you don't deserve." Remember Ron's passing by grace?

Mercy takes the same words used to define grace, with a little change. Mercy is "*not* getting what you *do* deserve." Read that again. Compare it to the meaning of grace.

Let me write out three mercy statements. Each is true. See if you can understand why I would call them mercy statements.

1. Millie disobeyed God's command, but He did not damn her.
2. Pastor Mueller made a lot of bad mistakes, but God gave him another chance.
3. Ron wasn't looking for God, but God kept looking after Ron.

I could change the names around a lot. Maybe instead of Millie, I could write *Eve*. Instead of Pastor Mueller, I could write *Adam*. Instead of Ron, I could write *Adam and Eve*. Then my three mercy sentences would be telling the story of the Fall from Genesis 3.

Why don't you read Genesis 3 again. Pick out some of the mercy-things that God did in that story. Be very specific. You will be surprised how many there are.

MINISTRY (MIN-is-tree)   *2 Corinthians 6:3*

If God brought St. Paul or St. Peter back across the years and plunked them down in your town before your church, do you believe they would recognize anything? Think about that, and answer these questions:

T   F   1. Peter and Paul would recognize a pastor because now some pastors wear a special collar, and other pastors are dressed in black or dark colors, and still others wear robes.

T   F   2. Paul and Peter would look at your church and immediately know that Jesus is worshiped there.

T   F   3. Paul and Peter would smile when the organ sounded, happy that the old familiar hymns are still being played.

The answer to all three of those statements is F, or false. They would know nothing about collars or robes or pastors like we have. Neither of them ever saw a church building and couldn't know what made a building "churchy." Hymns and organ music? Neither ever heard an organ or sang our familiar hymns, or anything like them.

But, one thing they would recognize right away. They would recognize Christians helping the poor, visiting the sick, comforting those in trouble, advising the mistake-maker. They would immediately know that *ministry* was taking place.

Ministry means "serving." Paul and Peter gave their lives to serving. They would watch for the serving things we do, and listen for the serving things we say. Based on what they saw and heard done in Christ's name and as a response to His call, they would recognize Christian ministry.

Make a list of ministry-actions your church does. And how about another list of ministry-words that your church says. Who does the acting? Who does the saying? Who ought to?

NEW TESTAMENT *Jeremiah 31:31*

If you ask most people about a New Testament, they are likely to start talking about part of the Bible. Those who know most will say that the New Testament is the last 27 books of the Bible. They will say it contains the four gospels (Matthew, Mark, Luke, and John) and lots of letters (epistles) written by different people. That's what they will say. And they are correct. The New Testament is part of the Bible. But the term, *New Testament*, means more than that.

I don't suppose that you have written a will. Have you? A will is a written document that states what someone wants done with their possessions after they die. A will is very important. We believe that it is so important that it cannot be changed. At least, it cannot be changed by anyone other than the person who wrote it.

The Bible contains two "wills." One was prepared by God many years before Christ was born. It is usually identified with the Law (remember that word?) and Mt. Sinai. The other also was written many years before Christ was born. Paul tells us in Ephesians 1 that God has had that second will ready from the beginning of time. Those two wills can be called testaments. The word *testament* means "will." A testament is the same thing as a will. So we can talk about the Old Will and the New Will as well as the Old Testament and the New Testament.

In the Old Testament, there are many signs and clear promises of what God would finally do in the New Testament. The true purpose of the Old Testament was to help all people see how desperately they needed something new and better. The New Testament spells out God's better plan.

So while we can say that the New Testament contains certain books of the Bible, it is much more than that. It's the teaching of God's new will for us, a teaching that is spread throughout the pages of Scripture. The New Testament was put in force by the wonderful thing Christ did. You can read about that in 2 Corinthians 5:19. In that verse, the word *reconcile* means that Christ straightened everything out between God and man.

Be aware that there are two uses of the term New Testament. To help keep that clear, do two things. Memorize the books of the New Testament. It shouldn't take you very long.

While you're at it, memorize 2 Corinthians 5:19.

If you do both of those things, you'll recall the difference between the two meanings and you'll be able to show the difference to your friends.

NUNC DIMITTIS (NOONK-dee-MIT-iss)   *Luke 2:25–32*

His name was Simeon. He had waited. He had waited so-o-o-o-long. At least, that's the way he felt.

We don't know exactly how the message came or when the waiting period started in his life, but the Spirit of God informed Simeon that the Promised One of God, the Messiah, would come during his lifetime.

Years passed. Simeon, the young man, became Simeon, the 40-year-old. More years slipped by. Still more years passed. Simeon becomes a very old man. He walks slowly. His voice is thin and squeaky. His hair turns white. But still no Messiah. No Christ from God. At least not as far as he knew.

Do you suppose Simeon ever said, "Could I be wrong? Did I dream that God promised to send the Messiah in my lifetime? Could it be a mistake? Maybe I should give up hoping and just die."

Whether he ever thought those thoughts, one thing was sure: he was getting old and nothing was happening!

One day there seemed to be an inner voice urging him to go to the temple. He had always obeyed those voices within himself. So Simeon hurried to the holy place. When he arrived, a young couple with a little baby was standing in the outer court. In that moment, God gave him to know that the little baby was the Messiah. Without a moment's hesitation, on the spot, Simeon prayed a prayer of praise.

We have a name for that prayer of Simeon. We call it the *Nunc Dimittis.* Just like the name for the Magnificat is taken from the first words of Mary's prayer in Latin, so the name *Nunc Dimittis* is taken from the first words of Simeon's prayer in Latin. Those two first words are "Now You let [me] go . . ."

We sing the Nunc Dimittis most often in the evening services we call vespers. Look through your hymnal's orders of service and see if you can find the Nunc Dimittis. When you find it, look over the words. If you can't find them in the hymnal, the same words are in Luke 2. Ask yourself, "Why does this seem to fit so well in the evening?" Could it be that it was spoken by a man who was in the evening of his life?

OLD TESTAMENT *Exodus 20:7—18*

What a mass of Israelites at the foot of Mt. Sinai! They had been led there from Egypt by Moses at God's command. A fence was built around that mountain so that no one would put their foot on that holy place. From the clouded peak thunder rolled and lightning flashed. Special people were permitted to meet God there. Others had to stay back. On that Mt. Sinai, the Old Testament was given again. It had been explained before, but at Sinai it was presented most clearly.

Remember that we said a testament is the same thing as a will? The Old Testament was God's first will for His people. God said, "If you will be my people (that meant live like He wanted), then I will be your God." He then spelled out what that would mean. *That* agreement was the Old Testament, the original will of God. It sounded so good. But it helped no one into heaven. It helped no one to heaven because no one could do what God asked.

I'm sure glad God had a second will! It is called the New Testament. Even though He gave a *New* Testament, that doesn't mean He changed in His desire that we walk in the way of the old one. Oh, no. If we could only live the Old Testament way this would be a better world for everyone. But we can't do that perfectly.

So while He didn't change in His attitude toward His Old Testament, He did show us another way of coming at His will. He sent His Son, Jesus Christ, to obey His commands for us. And then He sends us His Holy Spirit to lead us toward a closer and closer walk in His will.

So what about the Old Testament now? As the way of reaching heaven, it won't work. No one could satisfy it. No one can today. Everyone who tries to live a perfect life makes mistakes. But the Old Testament is still a very important thing to us. It keeps reminding us of God's will, of His forgiving mercy, and of better ways to live. All three!

The term *Old Testament* also refers to the 39 books that are in the first part of the Bible. Those Old Testament books contain a lot of New Testament love and mercy and grace and forgiveness and promise. Never forget that. But the term *Old Testament* can measure off those books that were written before the promise was fulfilled in Christ by His birth.

Name the first and the last book of the Old Testament. And while you're at it, name the one in the middle. Do it here:
1. _____ ;   39. _____ ;
20. _____ .

OMNIPOTENT (om-NIP-po-tent)   *Matthew 28:18*

I like the *o* words of our Christian faith. They may be tough to pronounce, but they are fun to say and exciting to understand. The *o* words are omniscient (om-NISH-shunt); omnipresent (om-knee-PRES-sunt) and omnipotent (om-NIP-potent). Those three words are among the many gifts given to us by the people who worshiped Christ more than 1,500 years ago.

As you recall, many earlier Christians spoke Latin, the language of Rome. The words about God that we get from those Christians are Latin flavored. Let me show you. Let's look at omnipotent.

Omnipotent starts with *omni.* That word, in Latin, means "all." It means *all* like "the whole thing," or "every bit of it." That's what omni means.

Now comes the other Latin-flavored part of the word: *potent.* Ever hear of the word *potent?* If you have, it was probably in a sentence like this: "That lady certainly wears potent perfume," or "You make potent cocoa." Potent perfume is perfume that is very strong. Potent cocoa has so much cocoa in it that it tastes a little bitter. Potent means strong. Now put those words together. What does *omni potent* mean? It means totally strong, or all powerful. *All* powerful and all *powerful.* More than Superman. Omnipotent can only mean God.

God can do anything He wants to do. Because He is omnipotent, He has
*Created the world and given life to man
* Fought and defeated the devil, Satan
* Planned our salvation and then made it possible for us to receive it
* Sent His angels to guard and protect His people

Let's cut out magazine pictures. Clip those pictures that show the power of God. Paste them together on a page of power. Under (or across) your collection of pictures, write in large letters our first "o" word: OMNIPOTENT.

OMNIPRESENT (om-knee-PRES-sunt)   *Psalm 139:7-10*

Omni means all. *Omni* potent equals "all powerful." *Omni* means the same thing in omnipresent. It means all.

And present? *Present* means present. Like, "Here I am." *Omnipresent* means present everywhere. Only God is omnipresent.

Only God is present everywhere, at the same time. He is present *everywhere, at the same time, all the time.*

An omnipresent God worries some people. They're not sure they want a God who's that close. Can He see everything we do? Can He hear everything we say? No, a God-Who-Is-Far-Off seems better to them. But when lightning hits around them; when bullets fly near their heads; when death and danger are on the prowl, they want God close. Frightened folks want a God-at-Hand.

People who want God close *only sometimes* have a way of blaming Him for most things. They like to say, "If God is close, why did we have the accident?" or, "Why did God let our little girl die?" or, "Why did God take my job?"

God is omnipresent. He does see the accident. He senses the danger. He watches us at work. But He gives *us* ways of handling those things. He lets us drive safer, use medicine, mind the business we have. God is present to help us do our thing.

Recognizing that God is present to help *us* face the task at hand helps us see Him differently. He's not a magic genie in a bottle who will come out when we rub the bottle and do the hard work for us. He doesn't whisper right answers in our ear so we pass a test. He doesn't wipe out sickness and eliminate death on earth. But He helps us study. He helps us take care of our bodies. When death comes as Satan's sure curse on us all, He steps on the other side of it and provides life eternal. He does this all because He is an omnipresent God and on our side.

It's important to remember God is *at* our side and *on* our side. One of His greatest names is Immanuel (Isaiah 7:14). The name means, "God with us." God is *with* us. The great additional news is that He is not only with us, He is for us.

Next time you get in a tight spot and need some help and strength, or when you feel a little blue, say and pray, "Immanuel." Use it as a statement of faith; a creed. And when you've said it, pause a moment. Figure out what God is trying to do *for you, through you,* that very moment.

OMNISCIENT (om-NISH-shunt)   *Matthew 6:25–33*

More than anything else in life, Lauren wanted to be a scientist. Scientists looked so glamorous. From TV she got the idea they walked around wearing white laboratory coats and carrying clipboards. They seemed so smart. She had watched as they dabbled with test tubes, peeked into microscopes, worked wonderful machines, studied bunny rabbits, and played with whirring computers. Even though she was only six, Lauren knew she wanted to be a scientist. At least that's the way she felt until . . .

One day, she told her daddy about her hopes. He asked a simple question: "Do you know what a scientist is? Do you know what a scientist does?"

Actually, she didn't know. She only knew what she thought they looked like. But she didn't really know what they were—or did.

How about you? Do you know what a scientist is? Do you know what that name means? Let's see how smart you are. Choose one of these answers. A scientist is (1) any person who wears a white coat, (2) someone who knows a lot, (3) men or women who sigh and say "Do I have to?" when asked to work, (4) people who like to ski.

Did you choose 2? If you did, that's correct. The word *science* (and *scientist* and *scientific*) comes from a Latin word that means "to know."

The word *science* is also the second half of our special "o" word for today. The first half is *omni*. That means all. The second half is *scient*. That means to know. Omniscient means to know everything.

Omniscient doesn't fit any scientist I know, but it sure fits God. He does know everything. The most important thing He knows is you and me (Isaiah 49:16). He also knows how much we need a Savior. Not only does He know of our need, He has answered our need. He gave us Jesus.

ONLY-BEGOTTEN *Matthew 3:17*

Billy was convinced Grandpa told tall tales. Sometimes. They weren't exactly lies. They were just strange stories. Grandpa's stories usually required a lot of believing—like the story Grandpa told about hunting when he was young.

Grandpa said that when he went hunting as a boy, his dad would give him only one bullet. Since the family needed only one duck or one rabbit for supper Grandpa got only one bullet.

Billy knew that if you are going to hunt with just one bullet, you better not miss. Grandpa never said whether he ever missed. He only told the part of the story about getting one bullet.

The word *only-begotten* is a kind of you-better-not-miss word, too. It's used about Jesus; *only* about Jesus. Only Jesus was only-begotten of the Father. Even though it is a one-time word, maybe we can unpack it a little for clearer understanding.

Only-begotten begins with the word *only*. Jesus is God's *only* Son. He is our *only* Savior. And He is the *only* way God has provided for our salvation. *Only* makes sense.

Begotten? That's the word Christians choose to describe what no one really understands. The Father and the Son and the Holy Spirit have always been. They weren't born. They didn't enter life like you and me. They always were. The word we use to describe the "always was" for Jesus is *begotten.*

I know we'll understand begotten better when we get to heaven. Or maybe we just won't worry about it there. Maybe it's the kind of word that gets us excited here on earth. Maybe once we're in heaven, we'll be having such a great time we'll not think a lot about it. But right now, take a careful look at it. It has beauty for us right here and right now.

For instance, God was so sure that His plan for salvation in and through Jesus Christ was the right answer that He provided no other. Jesus was the *only* begotten Son of God. Redeeming you and me through the cross is the *only* plan God had.

More than that, He's the only thing needed. If someone tells you that there is another way of being saved, don't you believe it. Read Galatians 1:8. Paul there nailed it to the wall: there is no other way.

I like what the Bible says about God's *only*. Find Acts 4:12b in the King James Version of the Bible and fill in the blanks: "There is _____ other name under heaven given among men whereby we _____ be saved." There is none. They didn't have to be any. None is needed.

P.

PALM SUNDAY   *Matthew 21:1–9*

That must have been some day! For once when Jesus came into town He got the royal treatment. Children and adults lined the streets. Palm branches waving. Hosannas! Running! Robes laid down as a pathway. That must have been some day!

I wonder why they call it Palm Sunday. Of course there were palms. We've already talked about that. Clustered in a bunch they were called *lulabs*. But it could have just as easily been called "Hosanna Sunday" or "Parade Sunday." There were lots of hosannas. And such a parade!

Or maybe they should have called it Passion Sunday. That's one of the ways we now describe it in our church year calendars. It begins Holy Week. After Palm Sunday comes Holy Monday, Holy Tuesday, and Holy Wednesday, days Jesus spent teaching. We've already talked about Maundy Thursday and Good Friday. That only leaves Saturday. It's called Holy Saturday. After that comes the first day of the next week, Easter Sunday.

Some week! There are actually more words written in the Bible about that week than any other week in Christ's life. This was a special week, one in which God's only plan for saving you and me was completed. It deserves to be spotlighted.

Well, whatever that special Sunday at the beginning of Holy Week might have been called, the name by which we know it is *Palm Sunday*, the Sunday before Jesus died. It's one week before Easter. It's the first day of Holy Week. It's all those things. and it's one of the few times in Christ's life that people really celebrated who He was.

Everyday in heaven is like Palm Sunday. Hallelujahs and hosannas billow around the throne of Jesus. Why wait? Palm Sunday reminds us that praising is a powerful part of our Christian life. There is no reason the praising can't start right now. So let's do it!

How? Draw a picture. Write a poem. Have a parade. Hum a

song. Make a pompon that praises Jesus. The children did that long ago. If it was good enough for them . . .

PARDON   *Isaiah 55:7*

Millie opened the newspaper and saw his picture right there on the front page. Such a big picture! It was the picture of a tired but happy man. Above the picture, in large black letters, stood the words, "Governor Pardons Smith."

Millie knew all about Smith. Smith had been accused of a murder, tried in court, and found guilty. She knew he had been sent to jail. She also knew Smith kept saying he was innocent. But the jury didn't believe him. The evidence seemed too much.

After a year in jail, a man turned up who confessed to the crime for which Smith had been jailed. That's when the governor acted. He pardoned Smith. Giving the pardon was as if the governor had taken a great eraser and erased everything that suggested Mr. Smith was guilty. Smith was pardoned. No more guilt. It was all gone. Taken away.

God pardons us. But He's better than the governor. He doesn't wait for someone to come and confess to our crimes. If He did, He'd wait forever. We're not innocent like Smith. We really have sinned. We have failed. We have made mistakes. We are guilty.

But the mercy and grace in the heart of God leads Him to pardon us anyway. He pardons by forgiving. (Remember the three meanings that word has?) He pardons by taking away our guilt, placing it on the Savior, and forgiving us.

Get some old newspapers. Check the headlines. Clip out words or letters needed to make this headline: *God Pardons Sinners.*

Maybe, instead of the word *sinners,* you may want to insert your own name. Paste those letters on a newspaper where the headline fits. Tape a picture of yourself under the headline. Now you can begin to realize what a wonderful and powerful word *pardon* is. And, good news! God pardons you.

PASSION (PASH-un)   *Acts 3:18*

Once Louise fell from her bike and really skinned her knee. That hurt. And once Louise suffered severe tonsillitis. That hurt. And once Louise was hit by a baseball. That hurt. But none of those hurts hurt like the hurt she felt when all the kids in the fourth grade thought she had stolen Sarah's dollar. They treated her like a thief. That really hurt. Deep. Louise cried.

It all happened so quickly. She had come back from recess a few minutes early. It was cold outside. Louise didn't feel well, so the teacher let her come in. In she came.

Everything was all right until Sarah entered the room, sat down at her desk and, a moment later, yelled out, "Who took my dollar?" Sarah looked right at Louise when she asked that horrid question. All the others looked at her, too.

But she hadn't taken the dollar. She said so. But do you think someone would believe her? Not really. No one believed her. Not then. All her classmates assumed that she had taken the dollar. That's the way it was until, later in the day, Sarah flipped open her book and out flew a dollar. Sarah had forgotten she had put it there just before recess.

Louise was relieved. Things got friendlier. Everyone said they knew she hadn't taken the dollar. But she would never forget the long hour of suffering she experienced that day before the dollar showed up. She would remember that hurt for the rest of her life.

Passion means intense suffering. When we talk of Christ's passion, we mean Christ's deep suffering on the cross. That suffering, plus everything else He underwent, is Christ's passion.

In Christ's passion He suffered beating. That hurt. In Christ's passion, He suffered a crown of thorns. That hurt. In Christ's passion, He was abandoned by His friends. That hurt. But the greatest and deepest hurt was the rejection He experienced from God as He hung on the cross. There, weighed down by all the sins of all people of all time was the real passion. That was the real suffering.

All that hurting and suffering—the pain, rejection, abuse, desertion—all that, together, is the passion of our Lord.

Some people don't like to talk about the passion. They want to forget. They don't like to think that He suffered. But if He did suffer through it all, can't we at least remember it? And, as we remember it, shouldn't we thank God for the gift of the suffering Savior and His passion?

How about writing a passion prayer? Pick out something that Jesus suffered and thank God that Christ went through that for you. That was His passion. But don't forget: His passion is your salvation.

PASTOR (PASS-tor)   *Jeremiah 3:15*

What do you call the person who is the spiritual leader of your congregation? Do you have a name for that one?

Many people call their spiritual leader the *preacher.* That title is common in the South. It pops up there in songs and in some poems. While preacher is not a bad name, preaching is actually only a part of what your spiritual leader does in serving you and others.

How about the *minister?* The word *minister* means to serve or help. Your spiritual leader certainly does enough of that!

I've heard people speak about their spiritual leader as the *reverend.* Have you ever heard that? That term is not proper English even though it is commonly used.

Parson? Have you ever heard of the term *parson?* That's an old title of great respect. A long time ago, in England the spiritual leader was called the *person.* Not parson. In the passing of time, the pronunciation and spelling changed from person to parson. That's how we got that term.

There are other titles for a spiritual leader: rabbi, chaplain, priest. But the title many spiritual leaders seem to like best is *pastor.* It has such a nice sound. It is a Latin word that means *"shepherd."*

Shepherds (or pastors) take care of sheep. They tend a flock. Throughout the Bible, the followers of God are sometimes called a flock. God is called a Shepherd. One of our favorite titles for Jesus is the Good Shepherd. And there is more about pastor/shepherd.

In the Bible, God asks His followers to choose their earthly shepherds, or pastors, carefully. He wants spiritual shepherds who will be like Him. He wants shepherds who will follow in His footsteps. He wants shepherds who will take care of His flock. That's why a good title for those who care for a flock like God wants it done is *pastor.*

Take a look at Psalm 23. Imagine Jesus as the shepherd in the Psalm. Look at the shepherding things Jesus does. He feeds and leads. Just watch Him. See if you can fit your pastor into that psalm, too. Good pastors usually fit pretty well.

PEACE   *Philippians 4:7*

Jesus had many names. Some of the loveliest are listed in Isaiah 9:6 Take a look at that verse. Find a name there that fits these blanks: P _ _ _ _ _ of p _ _ _ _ _ .

Now let's figure out the meaning of that title. First, ask, "What is a prince?" You don't need me to answer that, do you? I'm sure you know. If not, you can look it up in a dictionary.

And there's that other word, *peace*. The dictionary says peace is like "the absence of war," or "freedom from quarrels . . . unrest . . . disturbance." Those are two definitions of the word *peace*. But that is not all that the Bible means by peace. Let me describe the Bible meaning of peace to you. Describing can be just as good as defining.

Peace is when your outside world is just the way you like it. Do you like it brisk and snowy? Or do you prefer warm and sunny days? Peace is when you have it as you want. And it's when you've got all your homework done and you know you have done good work. Peace is feeling totally alive. No aches. No pains. No limps. And on top of it all, peace is when your mom and dad smile at you, telling you, and others, what a great blessing you are in the family! All that is peace.

And peace is more than that. It's also when you're getting along great with your friends (you like them and they like you) and when you know that God loves you and you have a place with Him in heaven. All that, put together, is what peace means. Peace means *every part of your life is in balance and everything fits.*

The way to get that inside/outside oneness is through Jesus Christ. He is the Prince of peace. He rules peace. He gives peace. Only He gives peace.

Almost every epistle St. Paul wrote begins with something about peace and the way you get it. Read the first few verses of Ephesians, Philippians, or 2 Thessalonians. Look for the word that leads to peace. Doesn't it say, "G _ _ _ _ to you and peace?"

If you claim God's grace toward you, you'll always have peace. Peace is God's grace alive and active in your life. When that's the way it is there is peace—in you.

PENITENT (PEN-ih-tent)   *Luke 15:11–24*

Have you ever seen a penitentiary? Sometimes they are called a state (or federal) prison. A penitentiary is a place where men or women are kept in cells, behind bars. It's a prison. But it's supposed to be more than that.

A penitentiary is supposed to be a place where people have time to become sorry for what they have done. They are put in a penitentiary to learn to regret their mistake. It is hoped that, after serving a sentence in the penitentiary, the prisoners will never break the law again. It is hoped that prisoners will become genuinely penitent.

Penitent? Let's see how good we are at describing penitent. We won't describe it in words. Let's draw the word *penitent.* Make a circle. Put in that circle the eyes, the eyebrows, the nose, and the mouth of a penitent person. Remember—a *penitent person.* Go ahead. Try it. Put together a face that looks penitent.

How did you do? Were you able to draw a penitent face? Let's check.

Do the eyebrows have a sad slant? Did you put tears near the eyes? Were the edges of the mouth tilted down? If that describes what you drew, I think you drew a face that looks penitent.

True penitence is more than an outward expression. There is inside feeling, too. There is an inner regret, an inner sorrow, an inner remorse, an inner sense of guilt, an inner anguish. You don't use all those words every day, and you may even have trouble pronouncing them. But you need to know there are a lot of words in our dictionaries intended to describe the feelings of penitence. Most are words that make you feel sad. Penitence is a sad word. At least it is in the beginning.

But there is another side to penitence, too. Penitent people can be on their way to forgiveness—if they ask. Then, when they receive the forgiveness that comes from their penitent beginnings, their whole face can change. Sad becomes glad.

Why don't you draw another face? Make the same kind of circle. Put in eyes, eyebrows, nose, mouth, and other features. Only this time, draw the face of a penitent person *who has been forgiven and who knows it.*

Always remember this: penitence can lead to something much better: forgiveness. And peace. And heaven.

PENTECOST (PEN-tee-kost)   *Acts 2:1*

Pentecost is another one of those great days of celebration sprinkled throughout our church year. It's like Easter and Christmas and Epiphany and Ascension Day. Pentecost fits right in among those great festivals. But it has its own special place. The word *Pentecost* gives us a hint.

Pentecost means "fifty" in Greek. Does that give you a clue? I'll tell you more. Before Pentecost was a Christian festival, it was a Jewish holiday. Pentecost was a harvest festival fifty days after the Passover. In the Holy Land, there are two, and sometimes three, harvests a year. Fifty days after the Passover is the end of the first harvest. People celebrated and rejoiced. The crops were in. Hooray!

Now it's time for you to figure things out. What Christian festival comes at the end of Passover? Think. Think of Maundy Thursday. Think of Holy Week. Think of all you know about Good Friday and things that happened on that day. Now, do you know the Christian festival that comes at the end of Passover? Did you say Easter? That's right! Easter.

Pentecost comes fifty days after Easter. The seventh Sunday after Easter is Pentecost Sunday.

The dating of Pentecost is not nearly as exciting as knowing what took place on the first Christian Pentecost. That story is written in Acts 2. You can read all the exciting details. Why don't you do that? And while you're at it, make a list of the surprising happenings of that day.

It's important to know the facts about Pentecost. It's even more important to know the meaning of those facts. Pentecost is not just a day for celebrating the early harvest. It is the day on which Christians celebrate the first coming of the Holy Spirit to His church. He came then. He came to stay. He comes to us now. He came then, and comes now, through Baptism and the Lord's Supper. He came then, and comes now, in the Word. In the Word? Yes! Ephesians 6:17 tells us that the Word is the s _ _ _ _ of the S _ _ _ _ _ .

Hooray for the coming of the Holy Spirit! Hooray for Pentecost!

PRAISE   *Psalm 148:2*

"What did you pay for that bike, Lee?" That was the first

question Kathy asked when she saw Lee riding his obviously new bicycle.

"A lot," answer Lee. "A lot." That's all he would answer.

"Did you pay $100?" asked Kathy. Lee's look pressed her on. "$200? $300? $400?" Lee's little nod caught her by surprise. $400! For a bike! Wow! And that's what she said. She said, "Wow!"

After that, Kathy told everyone about Lee's $400 bike. Once she knew how much it cost, she didn't stop talking about it. She described how pretty it was; how red it was; how light it was; how fast it was; how strong it was. It was the best bike she had ever seen. What convinced her was the $400.

There is a relationship between the story of Lee and his $400 bicycle and the word *praise*. Praise actually means "to price." Praising is pricing. Pricing means setting a price. A $1,000 ring is a super ring! A $20,000 van is some van! When you price, you praise. When you praise, you always suggest the price.

In order to get ready to praise God, let's first "price" Him. What's He worth? What's it worth that He hears you? $_____ . What's it worth that He protects you? $_____. What's it worth that He forgives you? $_____ . What's it worth that He opened heaven to you? $_____. Put dollar numbers in those blanks.

If you think that everything He does for you is worth a lot, you will praise Him a lot. If you don't think His blessings are worth very much, you won't praise Him much. It's as simple as that.

Just in case you wonder how much God "prices" you, consider this: the price He paid to make you His own was more than money. It was the life of His Son. You must really be valuable!

PRAY 1 Thessalonians 5:17

When I was a little boy (and sometime after I grew up, too), I thought prayer, and praying in church, was dull. Not *my* praying, mind you. The pastor's. I thought the pastor's praying was dull. I thought it was b-o-r-r-r-r-i-n-g.

It took me a long time to figure out why I felt that way. At first, I thought it was because I didn't like praying. Then I thought it was because I didn't like the pastor. The final understanding came out very different. I discovered I didn't like the praying of some pastors, because they used words I didn't understand, that I seldom used, and that I couldn't pronounce.

That's what started me thinking about Jesus' prayers. *I can understand them.* His words from the cross—such as "Father, forgive them, for they do not know what they are doing" (NIV)—are prayers I can understand. When He taught us to pray, He gave us a prayer I can understand. The words in the Lord's Prayer are simple and direct. I may not grasp all the meaning, but I get enough to make praying His prayer important.

Since then I started looking for clear prayers. I found a lot. Some are Psalms. When I've done something bad and need to be assured of God's care, I just love to pray Psalm 130. I pray it with power. And when things look tough, I pray through Psalm 23 or Psalm 46.

And I started paying attention to the short prayers in the hymnbook. Remember what we call them? Collects? I like them.

Praying that really satisfies me always sounds like two friends talking. One of them is listening. One of them is talking. The listener is God. The talker is me, or someone near me whose heart is as full of need as is mine.

Pray? I sure do. I like to talk to God. I even pray by writing Him letters. Talking or writing, I try to keep things simple. I use my language. How about you?

Why don't you write a simple prayer? Use your language. Write it the way you talk. Prepare it as a present for God. Do you think you could write one—and then pray it? Try.

PRELUDE/POSTLUDE   *Psalm 150*
Psalm 150 is sure some psalm! I can't believe all the musical instruments it mentions as suitable for praise to God. Tambourine and guitar—those are about the same as a timbrel (TIM-brell) and a psaltery (SAWL-tree). The other stringed instruments mentioned could be like a violin or a viola or a bass fiddle.

I once read Psalm 150 with a group of imaginative kids. Every time a musical instrument was mentioned, they imitated it. We blared like trumpets. We banged like cymbals. We had a great time and a lot of fun. We were serious in our intention, but smiled and laughed in our actions. That's what this Psalm suggests.

We do a lot of music things in church. Some of the best music in the world is played just as the service starts. There is other great music played as Christians leave after the service. We call those special music moments at the start of the service, "the *before* music," and the music after is called "the *ending* music." But we use a fancier name. The music before is called a prelude (PRE-lood), and the music after a postlude (POST-lood). The *pre* in prelude means "before." And the *lude* means "play music." So prelude means *to play music before*. I am sure you can figure out what postlude means, especially if you know that *post* means "after."

Christians take preludes and postludes seriously. They value them as a definite part of the worship service. The prelude is related to the whole worship service the same way a front porch is related to the house. And can you guess what the back porch of the worship service is called? Postlude, of course.

Music is one of God's greatest gifts to us. Only human beings can make music, or sing, or play musical instruments. Animals can howl and bellow away. Their noise sometimes sounds musical, but not really. Only man can consciously create that beautiful thing called *music*. It would be tragic if we could do something like that, but didn't.

Why don't you talk to your congregational organist, or pianist, about how a prelude or a postlude is chosen for each Sunday? Have your church musician play examples of preludes and postludes. Listen to how the music sets a mood in worship.

PROPITIATION (pro-pish-she-AY-shun)   *1 John 2:2 KJV*
John liked almost everything about his paper route. He liked the money. He liked the exercise. He liked meeting people. But one thing he didn't like. He didn't like Mrs. Norem's dog.

When he delivered her paper that dog would come running out of nowhere. The dog barked and snapped at his ankles. Mrs. Norem kept assuring him the dog wouldn't bite. John didn't believe her. John was scared of that dog. What could he do?

First, he thought he would get a stick and whack the dog. He even put a few rocks in his pocket to throw at the dog. But he didn't dislike animals. and what if the dog got meaner? Hitting the dog didn't seem to be a very good solution.

He decided on another approach. He asked his mom for the bone left over from the steak they had eaten last night. When he came to the Norems he tossed that bone to the dog. It made a difference. From that day on, he always tried to have something for the dog. One day it was a dog biscuit. Another, a bone. Everyday he brought some kind of a snack for the dog. He noticed that it barked less, it snapped less, and even seemed just a little friendlier. John didn't realize it, but he was *propitiating* that dog. He was doing something to make that angry dog happier.

The Bible tells us that God is angry with all sin. He doesn't hate the sinner. He despises the evil that sinners do. Why shouldn't He be angry? He created a perfect and sinless world. He wanted it filled with love and peace. But sin entered. And God became angry. what could possibly calm His anger over sin? What could *propitiate* Him?

Jesus Christ could propitiate Him. He is the propitiation for our sins. He came, lived in this world as one of us, and paid for the wrong we had done. His perfect obedience was a propitiation. He satisfied God. He brought out God's forgiving heart. He made God happy and gained forgiveness for us. Jesus was the propitiation for our sins.

Propitiation is a hard word. Say it five times, or until it slips out of your mouth right. It's a great and wonderful word to know. It's even a greater word to know about.

PULPIT (PULL-pit)   *Nehemiah 8:4a*

I have two reasons for asking you to look for a verse in the Book of Nehemiah. First of all, I wanted to see if you could find the book. Was it hard?

Secondly, this is the only verse in Scripture which contains the word *pulpit*. When you add up all the folks who were supposed to be standing on that pulpit with Ezra, it's clear that we today would probably call their pulpit a platform or a stage. And that's exactly what the word *pulpit* means. A pulpit is a raised platform or stage.

Remember our discussion about the chancel? We talked about where the altar is located. And the lectern. We discussed the communion rail and the chancel itself. But where is the pulpit in your church? Why don't you draw a plan of your chancel and mark where all the things are located: the pulpit, the lectern, the altar, the Communion rail.

Can you describe your pulpit? Some pulpits are very simple. Many are fancy. Some are decorated with carvings and words. Others are plain flat wood. Some are tall. Some are made of metal. Some are stone. What about yours?

Whatever the appearance of your church's pulpit, the purpose of the pulpit must always be kept clear. The pulpit is the platform from which the Word of God is spoken. Most churches insist that only the Word of God is spoken from their pulpit. When the pastor stands in (or on) the pulpit it must be for preaching to people a true message of God, "which [is] able to make [us] wise unto salvation through faith which is in Christ Jesus" (2 Timothy 3:15 KJV).

That the true Word of God is "inspiried by God" (2 Timothy 3:16) is also taught in Scripture. Those two quotations set the tone for what ought to be happening in any Christian pulpit. From the pulpit, we ought to hear the inspired story of our salvation. That story is to bless all who hear.

One of the nicest pulpits I have ever preached from had special words carved on the inside where only the pastor could see them. The pastor saw them while preaching. The words are from John 12:21. One translation reads, "Sir, we would see Jesus" (KJV).

The pulpit is the proper place for making sure that Jesus is seen. It's an improper place for anything else.

QUICKEN (QUIK-ken)   *Ephesians 2:5 KJV*
Ever had a splinter in your finger? Do you know what comes next? As a boy, that always first meant my mom or dad would

get some disinfectant *and a needle.* Then came trying to get the splinter out.

As that needle got close to my finger, I knew it was going to hurt. What did Dad say? "Hold still. This won't hurt." It won't hurt *him!* But me? That was different.

I did discover that sometimes as Dad was poking around, he was right. Sometimes it didn't hurt. Other times it stung as I felt the sharp point bite. When the needle nips you a little bit, and you can feel it, that's your signal the needle has touched the *quick.* The quick is the living and sensitive flesh of your body. When you touch it with something sharp, it will sting or hurt.

If quick is your living flesh, then *quicken* must have something to do with making it alive. That's right. If you quicken something, you make it respond; you cause a lively reaction.

The Bible uses the word *quicken* in two ways. First it uses the word to describe how God brings some people to faith by the Holy Spirit. There they are, dozing along through life, when WHAM! (just like at Pentecost) the Holy Spirit brings life. They are spiritually quickened.

The word *quicken* is also used to describe what God does when He brings dead people to life—like on the Last Day. He will quicken the dead. He will raise the dead and make them fully alive to stand before Jesus.

Both uses of the word *quicken* are wonderful. Both are important to the life of Christians.

I was first quickened when I was baptized in Springfield, Ill., in 1929. How about you? When were you quickened? _____ _____ . Where were you quickened? _____ .

I'm going to be quickened again when God sends His holy angels to blow the trumpet on Judgment Day. I'm going to like that quickening, too.

Which is better? I don't have to choose. One has happened already. The other surely will.

REDEEM (ree-DEEM)   *Galatians 4:4–5*

The greatest story of all time is the story of God's redeeming love in Christ. Nothing matches that story for beauty, for love, for care. Here's what happened.

In the beginning of history, God created the world and everything in it. Adam and Eve, too. When the creating acts were done, God said each time, "That's good" (Genesis 1:4, 10, 12, 18, 25, 31). The world and everything in it was perfect.

It stayed that way until sin showed up. But sin didn't just show up. Satan *brought* sin and Adam and Eve *bought* sin. From that time on, everything went bad. God's creation was no longer perfect. The world and everything in it had been contaminated (corrupted) by the devil.

But God didn't give up on His creation. He didn't go on to something more interesting. He didn't stop loving. Or caring. Man failed Him, but He would not fail man. He developed a plan for getting man back. Paul talks about it in Ephesians 1:3–11. Sometime you ought to go through that section of Scripture very slowly and think through all God did. Maybe make a list.

I can't tell you why He came up with His plan. I could guess. But I don't know. Maybe God will explain it someday in heaven. But I'm just as happy not knowing the why. I'm happy because I know the how. He decided to get us back with this "how": *He would buy us back.* He would pay the ransom to get us from Satan and defeat death and sin.

The ransom? The ransom was the life of His only begotten Son. God gave up Christ for us. He offered Him as the ransom in order to buy us back. Redeem means to "buy back."

Redeem is a wonderful word. It's an action word. But it can also be the name of someone. If you add a couple letters, you get one of our greatest names for Jesus: *Redeemer.* The Redeemer redeems. Jesus bought us back.

I'm sorry He had to leave heaven and come down to get us. I'm sorry He had to, but I'm glad, for our sake, that He did. He bought me again. I belong to Him. In 1 Corinthians 6:19–20, St. Paul tells us something very important about ourselves. He says, "You are not _____ _____ ; you were _____ with a _____." That's what redeem means. Bought. Bought, again.

REFORMATION (re-for-MAY-shun)   *Hebrews 9:13–15*

Jeannie liked it best when the teacher brought out the clay. Those next minutes in the classroom were wonderful. Jeannie would take her ball of clay and form all kinds of things: a dog, a fish, even a kitchen stove with pots on top.

Mrs. Fisher admired Jeannie's work. She would compliment Jeannie for her modeling skills. But there always came the sad time when modeling was over. She would wad up the things she had made, mold them into a lump, and put the clay back in the box. that was always a little sad. But Jeannie knew that another clay day was coming. She knew she would get her clay back. Then she could reform all her favorite things.

Reform. Reform means to take something, wad it up, put it away, then get it out and make something once more. *Reform.*

Clay can be reformed. By the power of the Holy Spirit, you and I can be reformed. Sometimes families and countries are reformed. Through abuse or neglect, they are lumped together into a blob. Later, through the efforts of someone who has the skill, they are reshaped into a new and better thing.

Would you believe that even churches have been reformed? They have. Every year, many churches celebrate a special time called Reformation Day. On that day we remember that Dr. Martin Luther tacked some statements and opinions on a bulletin board many years ago. It wasn't exactly a bulletin board, it was a church door; but that's the same thing. He wanted to discuss what the Bible said about how God's work should be done. When people started discussing, things started getting reformed. On the first Reformation Day, Oct. 31, 1517, people took Luther's suggestions so seriously that reforming change started. Even people who aren't Lutherans celebrate the day Dr. Luther tacked up his statements.

Every new generation in the church needs to look carefully at what they are doing. They need to review what they believe and why they believe it. A close study of the Bible, and their faith, may suggest it's time to do some reforming. But reforming isn't bad. If it's done under the Word, it will always be an improvement. Reforming beats continuously doing the same old wrong things.

Look for some reforms that have taken place over the years in church or nation or in your city. Identify a man or a woman who is helping reform take place. Check out what they are doing. Decide whether it's the kind of reform of which God will approve.

REPENT (re-PENT)   *Mark 1:15*

John the Baptist must have been some guy! You can read about him in Matthew 3, Mark 1:1–12, Luke 7:19–28, and John 1:19–37. By now, you should be Bible student enough to dig around and find some things by yourself. For instance, what does Scripture tell us John wore? _____

_____ .

What did he eat? _____

_____ .

How did people react to him? _____

_____ .

What finally happened to John (Matthew 14:1–12?) _____

_____ .

One more thing. What was John's best one-word sermon?

_____ .

Did you answer *repent*? If you did, you are correct. But what does that mean?

The word *repent means* "turn around," or "change your mind," or "be sorry enough to go back and redo things right." John told tough soldiers to repent. He said the same thing to troubled sinners, pious church people, and common folk. He said they all needed the same thing. They needed to repent, change their way, get ready to receive the goodness of God.

Christians are serious about repenting. They struggle every day to change their life so that it becomes more like what God wants. For them repenting is a kind of doorway to the great gifts of forgiveness and peace that God wants us to have. It starts when we admit we have done wrong and want to get right.

Did you know there are two special seasons in the year when the Christian church accents the word *repent*? Both of these

seasons rhyme with repent. Let's see you figure it out. One is
__ __ __ ent. The other is __ ent.

Did you write *Advent* and *Lent*? Those are the seasons. Advent is the repenting season four weeks before Christmas. Lent is the repenting season six weeks before Easter. During both times, Christians concentrate on changing, improving, doing things that mean walking closer to God. They repent.

No matter the season of the year, our *today* is always a good time for repenting, turning around, turning away, turning toward. If you're going the wrong way, turn around. If you're moving toward something bad, turn away. If you're looking for God's goodness, turn toward Him.

Say a "repent" prayer. Mine goes like this: "Turn me, Jesus. Straighten me out. Give me Your Spirit so that I may do things differently. In Your name. Amen."

RESURRECTION (rez-zur-REK-shun)   *John 11:25–26*

The saddest day in Tom's life was the day Grandma Morris died. It was as if someone had turned out all the lights in the world and painted everything gray. Grandma Morris was special to Tom. She baked cookies for him. She took care of him when his mom went shopping. Grandma Morris was the one who argued that Tom was old enough to have a bike. A lot of times, she gave him movie money. Now Grandma Morris was dead. She was gone. Tom would never see her again.

Christians say Tom *will* see Grandma Morris again! They don't just say it—they shout it. Jesus told Martha in John 11:23, "Your brother will rise again." To support His almighty words, He performed a miracle. It's a great story. You ought to read it. The best part is the exciting moment when Lazarus walks out of the tomb! He was resurrected. He had been dead. He rose again—alive!

Resurrect means *rise again*. 1 + 1 = 2. Rise + again = resurrection. Simple. What wasn't so simple was making a human resurrection possible.

The process began with Christ fighting Satan, the father of death. The story of how the devil gave us death is in Genesis 3. The story of how Jesus replaced death with life is in the gospels. Paul said, "Death is swallowed up in victory," and then, in 1 Corinthians 15:55–57, explained how that all happened.

Read that section. You've got to get it straight. These words will bless you all your life long.

Resurrect means *raise from the dead.* It means *raise again.* Christ makes the resurrection happen. He died and rose again first. John tells us that Christ's blessed victory is ours in John 3:16–17. Those resurrection words are so good they ought be memorized. I wonder how long it would take you to do that. Time yourself. See if you can memorize John 3:16–17 in 4 1/2 minutes. Ready? Start.

RIGHTEOUSNESS (RI-chuss-ness)   *Romans 4:3*

You've got to at least be *right* if you're going to be *righteous.* Righteous means more than being right. It means being right all the time.

Have you ever heard of anyone who is half right? There is actually no such thing. Half right is not right. It's wrong. Half healthy is not healthy. It's sick. Half good is not good, it's bad. Halfway home only means you have a long way to go. Righteousness is like that, too. It's no halfway word. Either you are righteous—totally—or you are not righteous—totally.

I know where that leave me. It leaves me on the wrong side of righteous. I'm not even half righteous. I'm less. That means I'm not righteous at all!

So what? What if I'm not righteous? What difference will that make?

Well, for one thing, unrighteous people make God angry (Romans 1:18). Unrighteous people make God angry because they fail to do His will. Their incomplete actions separate them from God—and from God's love—and from God's heaven. God doesn't push them away. They separate themselves. Do you remember how I talked about me? *I* am unrighteous. I am separated.

Since God only accepts righteous people, how will I ever get near Him? How will I ever enter His heaven?

Good news! What I cannot do (be righteous) God does for me. In one of our great hymns we sing:

"When He shall come with trumpet sound,
O may, I then in Him be found,
Clothed in His righteousness alone,
Redeemed to stand before the throne!"

If that isn't clear enough, in another hymn we claim:

"Jesus, Your blood and righteousness
My beauty are, my glorious dress."

Jesus gives me His righteousness. My righteousness is the righteousness He gives me. He designs and manufactures the clothes for my eternity.

Did you ever think about Jesus as a clothes designer? Did you ever think that a Christian wears designer clothes? Do you know whose name will appear on the hip pocket of our clothes of righteousness? And whose emblem is sewn above the shirt pocket of our spiritual knitwear?

Draw a picture of what someone would look like if they were dressed in the righteousness of Jesus. Add lots of Christian symbols. Pick the right colors.

SANCTIFY (SANK-ti-fie)   *Ephesians 5:25–27*

Smoke filled the room quickly. It was thick. Audrey could barely see the glowing light of the exit sign toward which she was crawling. Crawling. She remembered that if you stay near the floor in a smoke-filled area, you'll find the freshest air. Audrey wasn't trying to get out of the room. She was working her way toward the exit sign. She knew that next to the sign was a fire extinguisher and fire alarm. She believed that if she could get the fire extinguisher, she could slow down the smoky fire. And the fire alarm would bring help.

Now suppose. Suppose that when Audrey got to the fire extinguisher, she discovered that someone had played with it and emptied it—in fun. And suppose they had broken the fire alarm. Of course, there was a sign near the extinguisher that read, "For Emergency Use Only." But suppose the sign had been ignored. Then what?

Don't worry, though. Audrey found the extinguisher and pulled the alarm. She crept back with the extinguisher and slowed down the fire enough so that when the firemen arrived it was quickly put out. She was able to do what she had to do because no one had misused the alarm and the fire extinguisher. Everyone seemed to recognize that both were *sanctified.*

Sanctified? A fire extinguisher and fire alarm sanctified? In a very special sense, the answer is yes.

Do you remember the word *holy?* Do you remember that holy meant "set aside for a special purpose"? The word *sanctify* means "to *make* something holy." To *make* it special. And the way you make something holy is by respecting it and using it as a holy object.

The building owners had installed fire alarms and fire extinguishers. They marked them as having a special purpose. They put each in special little cases near the exits of the hall. They "set them aside for a special purpose."

The other people sanctified those extinguishers, too. They recognized their specialness. By their attitude and care of the fire extinguishers and the alarm, they sanctified them. They made them holy. Special.

God has sanctified us. He has set us aside for a special purpose. It is something He has done. Remember that if a word ends with *ify* (as in glor*ify,* magn*ify,* pur*ify*), it means that someone is doing something. The someone is God. His "doing" is sanctifying us. But how?

Let's let the Scripture tell us one way. John 17:17 (KJV) reads, "Sanctify them through Thy _____ ; Thy _____ is truth." When you fill in those blank spaces, you'll know one way that God sanctifies us.

SANCTUS (SONK-toos)   *Isaiah 6:1–8*

That vision of Isaiah in chapter 6 is really something. You almost need to draw a diagram in order to keep things straight.

Isaiah had a vision, or a dream. Was it at night? Maybe. Maybe not. He was standing outside of the temple looking in and what he saw was a glorious throne. The Lord was sitting upon it. All around Him were seraphim (SAIR-ra-fim), mighty, angellike creatures, with six wings.

Did you notice what the wings were for? Two were for _____ _____ , two were for _____ , and two were for _____ .

In all the excitement in this smoking temple room, other angels were flitting back and forth singing to each other, "Holy, holy, holy." That word, *holy*, in Latin is *sanctus*. In many worship services, a triple sanctus (or holy) is said or sung just before the bread and the wine of the Lord's Supper are blessed. The words, "Hosanna in the highest," are also used. The Sanctus comes from Isaiah 6. The hosanna comes from Matthew 21:9.

What was going on when the Sanctus was said by the angels in Isaiah's vision? And what could be the connection between the Sanctus (Holy, holy, holy) and the hosanna words in our worship?

The Sanctus in our worship is the signal in our worship that something very special, very holy, is about to happen. When the singing of the Sanctus is completed, the pastor blesses the bread and wine. He consecrates it (KON-see-krate). That means he asks God to set the bread and wine aside for a holy saving purpose. The added hosanna helps us know that is happening. Remember that hosanna means "save now?"

Lutheran Christians, and many others, believe that once the bread and wine have been consecrated, the Lord Jesus Christ is truly present and that, in a miraculous way, we receive His true body and blood. In receiving His body and blood, we receive Him. In receiving Him, we receive what He earned for us: forgiveness of sins, power for new life, and the hope of heaven. No wonder, at a moment like that, God's people join Isaiah's angels and sing, "Holy, holy, holy" (or we could just as easily sing, "Sanctus, sanctus, sanctus").

SAVE   *Matthew 8:25*
1. Save a dollar means _____ .
2. Save a life means _____ .
3. Save a dessert means _____ .
4. Save time means _____ .
5. Save expenses means _____ .
6. Save a soul means _____ .

The word *save* sure means a lot of different things! It can mean different things in the Bible, too. Sometimes it means to rescue a person from danger—as when Noah was saved by the ark or the disciples were saved by Jesus in the storm.

But most of the time, in the Bible, it means to pull people from the power of Satan and place them in the safe hands of the Lord.

Save is not a temporary help. To be saved by God is to be kept by Him forever. Jesus' saving power protects us until He comes again as our Judge and Ruler.

But why should God save anyone? The answer to that is in an amazing little word listed in Ephesians 2:8. It has five letters. Got it? The word starts with *g*. Got it? I'm sure you have. We are saved by *grace.*

I hope you'll never forget grace. When people forget grace, they forget why God saves. They even forget *that* God saves. They start thinking that God does His work for them because they are good, or intelligent, or wealthy, or American. Not so. God saves us by grace (undeserved favor) through faith in Jesus Christ. It's that simple. It's that complicated.

By the way, there's another word that is almost like save. That word is *salvation.* Salvation and save are the same. Both mean to be kept safe. When you have salvation—when you have been saved—you are kept safe in the hands of the Lord.

SERMON (SUR-mun)   *Matthew 5:1-2*

Remember what the word *bible* means? It means book. The word *sermon* is just as direct in its meaning. Sermon means speech. A sermon is a speech.

But a sermon is not just any kind of speech. A sermon is a speech that explains or teaches something about God. It is usually based on words from the Bible. The speech the pastor gives in the worship service each week is called a sermon.

Can you remember last week's sermon in your church? What was it about? Think. If you have trouble remembering, decide that you will pay special attention next week. Then, next week, see if you can complete a sentence that begins: "The sermon this Sunday was about _____

_____.

If you have difficulty with that sentence, talk to your pastor. He will help.

I think the best sermon ever preached is recorded in Matthew 5, 6, and 7. It is called the Sermon on the Mount. Take a look at Matthew 5 and see if you can answer these questions about that sermon:

1. Who was the speaker? _____.
2. Nine times the preacher said certain people were *blessed.*What does blessed mean to you? Pick an answer from these choices: (a) you are special; (b) I love you; (c) wonderful things will happen to you. (Did you pick all three? I did. I think blessed means all those things, and probably some more, too.)
3. What does He mean when He tells you that you should be salty salt—and a lit light? Put your answer here:

_____ .

You can read the rest of that sermon and ask more questions of yourself. It won't take long. The words are clear. I suspect you'll read them many times in your life. Each time you read His sermon, you'll find something new. His words prove there are sermons which can be very helpful.

SERVICE/SERVE   *Matthew 10:42–45*

What a way to start the day! The room was cluttered and dirty. Yesterday's chalking still marked the blackboards. The wastebaskets were filled to overflowing. The erasers? They were so dusty that when someone tried to use them the chalky powder puffed out and half the class coughed. That's not all.

The floor was a mess. No one had swept up the dirt tracked in from the playground yesterday afternoon. Desks were still sticky from the spills and drips of the birthday party for Elaine. The pencil sharpener was full of grindings. All the paper was gone. The room was cold, and water from last night's rain had leaked onto the windowsills. Who could start a class under those conditions?

But it wasn't the conditions that caused the difficulties. The difficulty was that no one had cleaned up those "conditions." When there is nobody to clean up, things stay just as bad as they are when they are at their worst.

What that classroom needed was a servant—a plain old-fashioned servant. It needed someone to tidy up and bring order; someone to empty and fill and wash and sweep. Then happy school could happen. But only then. When the servant arrived and serving started, things could work well.

School isn't all that needs serving and a servant. The whole world needs serving and servants. It can't get along without both. When there are no servants, or no servants who serve, the world gets messy. Servants make room for good things to happen.

But don't be fooled. Servants don't usually look like servants. They look just like ordinary people. They go about their serving doing the things needed to keep life orderly. Some servants are disguised as teachers. Others look remarkably like parents. Some appear as pastors. Others are electricians, builders, sweepers, healers, sellers, and all kinds of other folks. They are the servants who make life work. You usually only notice them when they aren't there.

List five servants (other than those I've already mentioned) who keep order in your life. Think about it for a moment. List five who make life livable. _____

By the way, is Jesus on that list? Are you?

SIN   *Luke 5:8*

The word *sin* can mean any of three different things. It can mean rebel, revolt, or miss the mark. Sometimes, it means one of these things. Sometimes, it means another. Each meaning illustrates and explains another terrible thing about sin.

When sin means to *rebel*, someone has refused to obey. The prisoner in jail who refuses to obey the guard is rebelling. A rebellious boy won't listen to his mother or dad. A nation in rebellion is one that refuses to follow the orders of its government. A rebellion took place in the United States soon after George Washington became president. Some Pennsylvania farmers refused to pay a tax to the government on corn they had made into whiskey. Their refusal was called "The Whiskey Rebellion." Their actions explain what the word *rebellion* means.

Revolt is something different. If you revolt, you not only refuse to obey, you want to get rid of the person who told you what to do as well. That happened in 1775 when the American Revolution began. The 13 colonies refused to obey the laws of the king of England. In addition, they replaced him with their own elected government and raised an army to drive the representatives of King George out of the country. That's why we call it the American Revolution and not the American Rebellion.

Rebel and revolt are serious explanations of what sin can be. When God tells us to do something, and we refuse, our sin is one of rebellion. When God tells us to do something, and we not only refuse to obey but reject God as well, our sin is that of revolting.

Throughout the Bible there are stories of people who rebelled and revolted. For instance, remember the revolutionary story of the golden calf (Exodus 32)? God did not immediately destroy them. He allowed Moses to call them back from their sin and save them. Mercy and grace were set into motion.

Our whole world rebels and revolts against God. But God does not send Moses. He has another plan. His plan for saving sinners today is sending the Lamb of God, Jesus Christ. Christ paid for our sins and offered this payment on behalf of all who accept it. He sends the Spirit to bring us back to our senses. He forgives our rebellion and revolting. He forgives our sin. What a caring God!

We've already discussed rebel and revolt. The other word for sin is very important as well, like "make a mistake" or "miss the mark." Let me tell you a story about that.

There was a time long ago when a group of explorers on a trip to the North Pole ran out of food. They needed food to feed their dogs and themselves. One of the explorers spotted a polar bear. He took careful aim and fired. He didn't kill the bear. He wounded it. The angry bear rushed at the explorers, tore up what was left of their camp, badly wounded their few remaining dogs and nearly caught them! Missing the mark got them in real trouble. Only a miracle finally saved them. When you try to be good, or try to help, or try to say the right things, and don't, it has very serious consequences. If you "miss the mark," you can hurt and do damage. Sin often means to "miss the mark."

Stop and think about the three meanings of sin. come up with an example from your life for each meaning. Remember when sin (in all three styles) brought harm, or pain, or took away joy. Sin always does that. Sin never builds or improves. It destroys. It damages wonderful things like fun, friendship, trust, even health. It does this even when you don't intentionally do wrong. that's why my next sentence is so important: God sent His Son to forgive our sins.

Remember what forgive means? Three things. If you've forgotten, look them up. The three meanings of forgive more than satisfy the three meanings of sin.

SOUL   *Psalm 103:1*

"Sit down, Grandpa. This is too much for you. I'm sorry I talked you into playing ball. I sure didn't want you to get hurt!"

That's how Steve tried to comfort his grandfather after a disastrous few minutes on their driveway basketball court. Grandpa had agreed to play with him. Very quickly it was apparent Grandpa couldn't move very well. He wasn't as well coordinated as Steve or Steve's friends. He ran out of breath—fast. He puffed. He turned a little red.

"Don't apologize," answered Grandpa. "I'm all right. Give me a moment. You know, on the inside of me, I can still play basketball like I used to. I can play just as well now as I always did. Inside. But my outside is different. My legs don't work the way they used to. I can't shoot the ball the way I used to. I can't run the way I used to. On the inside, I'm still 17. On the outside, I'm an old man."

Grandpa understood that there is an "outside me" and an "inside me." Everyone has both. When you are young and full of strength, the two look and act alike. But as you get older, the two "me's" begin to separate. The outside me gets wrinkles and slows down. It can get smarter, too. But there are growing differences between the inside me and the outside me as we grow old.

That inside me is what I think the Bible means by soul. It's the real me. It's the one that knows me best and never seems to age. It goes on year in and year out. Jesus died to save my soul—the inside me. In the judgment, my inside and outside will be united again. Both are important.

In the meanwhile, I must take care of my soul. I want things to go well with my soul. If I hurt my soul, I hurt the very heart of me. and who would want to do that to themselves?

The real me. Think about your real me. Write a paragraph describing it. What's your soul like? If you didn't tell, would people know?

SPIRITUAL (SPEER-rit-chul)   *1 Corinthians 15:44*

Pinch yourself. Go ahead. Do it. Not hard. Pinch yourself a little and ask yourself: "Am I real?" Are you?

"Of course," you would say. "I'm real because I felt the pinch. I reacted to the pinch. Besides, I can see me. I'm here. I'm real."

St. Paul would agree with you. He would say that you were seeing and feeling your natural body. Your natural body is you. Really. "But," St. Paul would say, "there is more."

There is more to you than body. There is *thought.* (That's real, but ever try to pinch a thought?) He would say there's *feeling.* (That's real, too, but ever tried to draw a feeling?) He would say there's *soul* (real—*real*, real!). All those things are as real as your natural body. But they can't be felt or photographed. Paul would call those things, which you know to exist as surely as your fingers and toes do, your *spiritual body.*

For Christians, the word *spiritual* has to do with the things that are more inside us and are usually brought by the Holy Spirit. The *spiritual* includes the soul, feelings, attitudes, thoughts, sensitivities, and all those other gifts of the Spirit listed in Galatians 5:22–23.

Look carefully at those verses from Galatians. With those verses before you, follow down a little checklist of things which are real in your spiritual self. They won't always appear the same to those outside. But you will know them on the inside. You be the judge. See if you have them. Here they are: _____ love, _____ joy, _____ peace, _____ patience, _____ kindness, _____ goodness, _____ faithfulness, _____ gentleness, _____ self-control. Those are spiritual blessings to us. God says they are gifts to Christians, so you must have them. Are some still wrapped?

Not every natural body looks alike. Not every natural body does things in the same way. Spiritual bodies will differ too. But they will differ within the boundaries of Spirit-given spirituality. No one is 100 percent blessed with all there is of those spiritual gifts. But God will bring some of all of them to you. He will help you develop each even more.

You are spiritual, Christian. You *are.*

STOLE   *Revelation 7:29*

Pastors wear special clothes at different times. When I'm

going to conduct a funeral, the children in school always know it. They see me wear a certain suit and know I will be having services for someone. Some pastors wear different collars, or a noticeable shirt, or a black suit. Those clothes attract attention and tell something about what a pastor is and does.

When the pastor serves in the chancel, there are *more* special clothes. We've talked about the flowing white robe called an *alb* (alb means "white"). A white robe ought to be called an alb. Right?

Some pastors wear a black under-robe called a cassock (KASS-sok) and a white over-robe called a surplice (SUR-pliss). Some wear crosses or medals that honor Christ. And many pastors wear a *stole*. It's pronounced as it looks.

The stole is a long band of cloth worn around the neck of the pastor. The two ends of the band reach down to the knees. A stole often has beautiful decorations sewn on it. The color of the stole changes, depending on the time of the year. About half of the time the stole is green. That's the color for the season of the year between Pentecost and Advent. That season lasts longest, from early June to late November.

Once a year, on Good Friday, the stole is black, a sign of sadness.

During Lent and Advent the stole is purple or violet. In Advent, it also might be blue.

Christmas and Easter bring out the white stoles. Sometimes a gold stole (reminding us of royalty and riches) is worn during these particular times of the year.

On special church festivals and on Pentecost, the stole is colored red. Red is the color of martyr's blood, and of the fire of the Holy Spirit. When we remember the church and growth and powerful witnesses, we see red.

The stole itself is worn as a sign of the pastor's responsibility. Only pastors wear a stole. It was originally designed to look something like the yoke that Jesus talked about in Matthew 11:28–30. Nowadays it is another sign that a pastor has accepted the duties of the servant and is ready to minister to the people.

Ask your pastor to see his stole. Sketch one of the symbols from your pastor's stole. Explain it. If you need help, ask someone, but most are obvious.

SUNDAY   *Matthew 17:2–8*

I like to spell it Sonday. That's not entirely wrong. The reason we have church on Sunday is because God's Son did something wonderful on a Sunday. Let's see if you can choose what it was: _____ (a) He completed His first house on a Sunday; _____ (b) He rose from the dead; _____ (c) He caught 493 fish in the River Jordan. The answer? It's *b*. And that's why sometimes I like to spell it Sonday.

But that's not the only great thing that happened on a Sunday. Scripture says God rested after creation on the seventh day of the week. That would be Saturday. If He rested on the seventh day, He must have started work on the first. That would mean the first day of God's work of creation was a _____ . Did you write the word *Sunday*? You are correct.

On the 50th day after Easter (you remember we call that day Pentecost), the Holy Spirit filled the disciples and gave them power to preach the truth and claim many for the kingdom of God. The 50th day after Easter is also a S __ __ __ __ __ ! Agree?

Three great things! Each happened on Sunday! Each honors one person of the Triune God. On Sunday, the *Father* began creation. On Sunday, the *Son* rose from the dead. On Sunday, the *Holy Spirit* came upon the disciples and started the Christian church. Any one of these great things would have made Sunday special. All three happening on this day (though many years separated) makes Sunday super special.

The early church agreed. When they discussed the day on which to worship each week, they settled on Sunday. They could think of no better selection.

When I forget my privilege and don't worship Him on Sunday, it becomes Sinday. But when I confess my mistake and ask Him for forgiveness, that Sunday becomes Sonday. And when I really get all tied up in worship and praising and praying and singing, every Sunday becomes a Funday. Sunday, Sinday, Sonday, Funday.

SYNOD (SIN-ud)   *Acts 2:46–47*

I admit it: *synod* is not a very common word. Other than among church people, the word is seldom even heard.

The most common use of the word *synod* is in a church's

title, like The Lutheran Church—Missouri Synod; or the Maryland Synod of the Lutheran Church in America. The first use refers to a large national Lutheran organization. The second to a smaller unit within a national Lutheran organization.

Synod comes from a combination of two Greek words which mean "the same road." When two or more people are walking down the same road, they can be called a synod. The word *synod* suggests agreement and friendship and unity.

The early Christian church was a synod. They shared everything. They shared possessions, eating, praying, worship. They even lived together. They made every part of their lives a synod.

Later in the history of the church, synod was used to describe a kind of church gathering to which people came from all over Europe for discussing important matters. They called those gatherings *synods.*

Even if we don't use the word very much, we ought to know something about it. Let me list a few sentences that describe some part of the word *synod*—

1. When you are in a synod with someone, all will agree with one another on most major issues.
2. When you are in a synod with someone, that means you are working together toward a common goal.
3. When you are in a synod with someone, you will try to co-operate before going off on your own.

All three of those sentences are correct. Each tells us something about a synod.

Tuck the definition of this word away in your mind. It will pop up every once in a while. You will know what it means.

TALENT   *Matthew 25:15—28*

Remember those homonyms? Write/right. Boar/bore. Bear/bare. Tale/tail. Two/too/to. Can you think of some homonymns that I haven't mentioned? Well, here's another almost-homonym, like one we had earlier. Remember confess? This hom-onymlike word has the same spelling, but two different meanings. The word? *Talent.*

In one of its meanings, the word *talent* is an ancient measure of money. It was like the word *dollar.* Jesus told a story of a man who gave five talents to one servant, two talents to another, and one talent to a third. That story is in Matthew 25. Read it. If you're by yourself, think about that story. If you're with some-one else, talk about it. Answer the question, "What's the point of the story?"

For me, the story is about how God lets people use His things. He expects them to use His things wisely and well. And He expects them to remember whose they still are.

But talent can mean something other than a measure of money. It is also a term to describe any special ability a person has, like the ability to play piano or paint, to do complicated math in your head, to shoot a basketball, or to compose music. Those special abilities are *talents.* People are born with them. Talents still have to be improved, but some people have the "something" with which to work from the very beginning of their life.

Christians believe that God gives special abilities. He gives them to people of His choosing. When He gives a talent, He expects it to be used to His glory and for the good of all.

Stand in front of a mirror. Take a careful look at yourself. Think before you answer. What talents do you have? They don't have to be better than anyone else's. But they *do* have to be recognized as special gifts from God to you.

I know a man whose talent is whittling, and another whose talent is whistling, and another whose talent is making stained-glass ornaments. All three of them recognize their talent and are willing to tell you that it came to them from God. All three have worked hard developing their special ability.

A person should do three things with his or her talent: (1) Thank God for it. (2) Develop it further. (3) Use it.

TE DEUM (tay-DAY-um)   *Psalm 103*

You guessed it. More Latin. By the time you finish this book, you're going to know a lot of Latin. That's good. Latin is the language that gave us many of our English words. It was also the language of the Christian faith until the end of the Middle Ages. To know a little about Latin is to know a lot about language.

So far, you have met the Latin background words for *alb, Nunc Dimittis, omniscient, Magnificat,* and many others. As you think of those words, add this one to your list: *Te Deum.*

The first thing you want to know is that *Te Deum* is only two-thirds of a more complete phrase, "Te Deum Laudamus" (lau-DAH-mus). Those three words mean, "We praise You, God." It's the title given to one of the oldest love songs in history. No one person wrote it. A lot shared in the preparation. Somewhere around the fifth century, A.D., the Te Deum was completed. Just listen to the words:

We praise you, O God, we acknowledge you to be the Lord;
all the earth now worships you, the Father everlasting.
To you all angels cry aloud, the heavens and all the powers therein;
To you cherubim and seraphim continually do cry:
Holy, holy, holy, Lord God of Sabaoth,
Heav'n and earth are full of the majesty of your glory.
The glorious company of the apostles praise you;
The goodly fellowship of the prophets praise you;
the noble army of martyrs praise you;
the holy Church throughout all the world does acknowledge you:
The Father of an infinite majesty, your adorable true and only Son, also the Holy Spirit, the Counselor.
You are the King of glory, O Christ,
you are the everlasting Son of the Father.
When you took upon yourself to deliver man,
you humbled yourself to be born of a virgin.
When you had overcome the sharpness of death,
you opened the kingdom of heaven to all believers.
You sit at the right hand of God in the glory of the Father,
We believe that you will come to be our judge.
We therefore pray you to help your servants,
whom you have redeemed with your precious blood.
Make them to be numbered with your saints in glory everlasting.

Christians have always loved to sing that song. Looking at

the words, you can figure out why. What a wonderful hymn of praise!

But Christians aren't the only ones who love praising God. God's people of every age praise Him. Take another look at Psalm 150. That writer knew about praise. And read the song of Miriam in Exodus 15:21, or the Magnificat (Luke 1:46–55) of Mary. Those wonderful followers of God knew about praise.

Let's praise God right now! We'll use the Te Deum for praise. We'll say it antiphonally (an-TIF-fon-nal-lee). That means back-and-forth. One person reads one verse, or half a verse, and another person responds with the second half.

Find someone to read the Te Deum with you. Be sure you read the words with excitement. They were prepared to be exciting. For most Christians, they surely are. How about you?

TEACH   *Matthew 28:20*

It isn't easy to teach. First you have to *know* something. Then you must know *how* to teach the something you know. That's still not all. If you know something to teach and you know how to teach it, there must be *someone* to learn. No teaching has happened until someone has learned. Teachers need learners.

Teaching is like making a fire. You gather wood and mound it. You pile little splinters and twigs at the base of that mound. You light a match and stick it right in the middle of it all. But if nothing starts to burn, there will be no blaze. If nobody learns, there is no teaching.

Jesus was a great teacher. He not only knew and taught His subject well, He helped His learners learn. He did this by teaching through helpful stories, for example. Remember His story about the boy who talked his dad into giving him his share of the inheritance, and then went off and wasted it? Remember how the boy came back? You can read that teaching-story-that-helped-learners in Luke 15:11–24.

Jesus taught by using everyday objects, like a fishing net (Matthew 13:47), some seed (Matthew 13:31–32), and powerful yeast (Luke 13:21).

He taught by telling about weddings (Matthew 22:3–14), pearl trading (Matthew 13:45–46), and family problems (Matthew 21:28–31). He used every method available. Jesus really was a great teacher. He was such a great teacher that people actually called Him that. They called Him Teacher, with a capital *T*. Can you guess which of the following names means teacher? Is it (a) Rabbi, (b) Messiah (c) Immanuel?

Did you choose *a*? You are correct. Rabbi means teacher. In John 3:2, the words *rabbi* and *teacher*, referring to Jesus, are combined in the same sentence.

Is Jesus your teacher? It depends. It depends on whether you are learning anything from Him. Are you? If you are, He is your teacher. To show if He is your teacher, write two things you have learned from Him. That should be easy. Two. Only two. Prove He is your teacher, learner.

TEMPT   *James 1:13*

Tempt must not be a very good word. Otherwise, why would Jesus tell us to pray, " . . . lead us not into temptation" (Matthew 6:13)? No, tempt is not a very good word. Leo learned that.

Leo loved bows and arrows. He made drawings of them in his notebook. He built them out of sticks and string. He could hardly talk without bringing up the subject of bows and arrows.

But the ones he made weren't very good. And there wasn't a lot of satisfaction just drawing a bow and arrow. He wanted to own a real bow and arrow. The ones he saw at Sears were beautiful. Everytime he got a chance, he walked through the sporting goods department and yearned for a good bow and some straight arrows.

He was convinced there was no chance for him to get either, though. Not soon, anyway. Leo was broke. Leo just couldn't hang on to money very long. He spent it. Fast. So how was he going to get that bow? Or the arrows?

Leo carefully considered three ways.

First, he consider stealing. Stealing went through his mind. But he decided against that approach. His conscience bothered him. He also realized that a bow and arrow were too large to hide under his coat.

His mom suggested that he work and save his money. That would take six months. Too long!

The third way was even more frightening than the first. He thought about taking the money for his sister's bank. He thought about robbing her.

What should he do? Leo struggled. He was tempted to do

number one and, then, number three. Even though he realized stealing was wrong—whether it was the bow and arrow or his sister's money—still he was tempted.

It would have been easier for Leo if he would have just turned his back on the stealing and put that out of his mind. If he would have realized that was not the way to do it, his final decision would have been easier. But he wrestled a long time. Once or twice, he almost decided to take it. Finally, after a long while, strengthened by his trust in God, Leo made a decision. No matter how long it would take, he decided he would work for the money and wait for the bow and arrow. He said to himself, "I'm no thief, and I don't want to become one."

When Leo shut the door of his heart to even considering wrong, and got busy saving some money, he wasn't tempted anymore. Leo realized God hadn't tempted him. Leo had tempted himself. He could very easily have said no right away. But as long as he was undecided whether he would obey God or his own inner urgings, Leo was being tempted.

I think the best way God has for leading us past temptation is by teaching us to use a simple two-letter word. That word is *no*. Say seven no's. Listen to their sound. Learning to appreciate the power of no is one of life's great thrills.

THANKSGIVING   *1 Timothy 4:4*

When we think of Thanksgiving, we think of the Pilgrims. They, supposedly, started Thanksgiving. One nice thing about the Pilgrim story is that they remembered God *even after things got better*. As a matter of fact, that's when Thanksgiving Day started for them. It started after they didn't lack food any longer.

Do you remember how bad things were for the Pilgrims? At one time, they came so close to starvation that the daily sharing of corn was only five kernels per person. That's not much. Today some descendants of the Pilgrims put five kernels of corn on their plates at Thanksgiving. When the family gathers, they hold those kernels in their hand and think about how God took care of their ancestors. As they lift each kernel, they recall some blessing of God from their far past, or their near past. They think of good things that happened to their great-great-great-grandparents. They think of good things that happened to them. *Then* they say thanks.

I don't suppose it's really Thanksgiving Day today, is it? Maybe where you are, but not here with me. So, do you think we can still be thankful even though it's not Thanksgiving Day? Let's try.

Take some little pieces of paper. Or maybe you can use some popcorn. Place a little mound of kernels or paper before you. Five? Say something you are thankful for as you lift each one. What five things come to mind?

My list of five things includes a wonderful family (my wife, children, son and daughter-in-law, grandchildren, brothers, sisters, parents—whew! What a lot!); then there is the church in which God has placed me as a pastor; our United States and all that means for me as a citizen; I like the things I own and use which God has given me; best of all, I claim with thanksgiving my saving faith in Jesus Christ. That's a lot to be thankful for. And there could be more.

Tomorrow, I'm sure I will think of other things. You just read my thanksgiving list for today. What does your thanksgiving list for today look like?

You know what comes after thanksgiving? Thanks*living.* Do you know what makes thanksgiving live?

TRESPASS   Ezekiel 14:13

NO TRESPASSING! That's what the sign said. And that's what the sign meant. There was to be *no trespassing*. Those two words on that sign told everyone that they should not pass through that man's land. No one was to pass.

One reason people put up those No Trespassing signs is that people do trespass. They pass through other people's property anyway. I suspect that most No Trespassing signs are placed at the very spot where most folks pass through. While the signs will caution the careful, they won't do much to stop a determined or willful trespasser.

And where else do you see the word trespass other than on signs? It's part of our religious conversation. Some translations of the Lord's Prayer teach us to pray, " . . . forgive us our trespasses as we forgive those who trespass against us." Other versions are a little different: " . . . forgive us our debts as we forgive our debtors."

The meaning of those two words (trespasses and debts) are

almost interchangeable. But not quite. Trespassing is an intentional act. So is borrowing that leads to being in debt. Trespassing makes us responsible to someone. So does borrowing. The difference is that trespassing always means breaking a rule or an agreement. Borrowing only *may* mean that. It may.

Serious trespassing took place between man and God. Man was the trespasser. Man walked right through the places where God intended no trespassing. Man walked right through God's idea of marriage and family and personal property and worship and changed each. Man trespasses on other areas where God says we should not push through. Man trespasses and brings all kinds of hurts to himself and others.

But there is good news. Trespassers who confess their sin to God can receive forgiveness. He took their pushy errors and harmful mistakes and nailed them to the cross where His Son died. The death of Christ is the propitiation (remember that word?) for the trespasses and trespassers.

The further nice thing about His forgiveness is that when we are forgiven, and Christ lives in our hearts, the Holy Spirit comes, who can turn us around and help us walk nearer God's will. The Spirit helps us resist the temptation to trespass on God's precious properties. He strengthens His own to live fuller and finer lives. That's the way God wants to deal with trespasses and trespassers. If only they will let Him.

TRIUNE (tri-YOON)   *2 Corinthians 13:14*
                                        Numbers 6:22-26

There's no way to define *triune*. It's like only begotten. Who knows exactly what that means?

Triune is such a strange word though. It's an impossible imaginary word like *hotcold* or *updown* or *plusminus* or *inout*. Things can be hot *or* cold, up *or* down, plus *or* minus, in *or* out. But they can't be both. Not at the same time. But triune is.

Triune means *threeone*. Three and one. Both. At the same time.

My head tells me that something can be three. It tells me something can be one. But it also tells me nothing can be *threeone*. But God's Word tells me that He is *threeone*. He is Triune.

Whether people think triune is possible or not, the church has long claimed that *threeone* is a fact. For the church, it is an old fact. *Threeone* goes back to the Book of Genesis: "Then God said, 'let us make man . . .' " (Genesis 1:26). Christians believe that *us* is the Father, the Son, and the Holy Spirit. *Threeone*. Aaron was instructed to bless his people with a three-part benediction: Numbers 6:24–26. Count them. We believe those three parts are references to *Threeone*, the Trinity.

There are many diagrams and symbols for the Trinity. The most common is a triangle with equal sides. Another is three circles of identical size, linked. These are ways of saying the Father is not the Son; the Son is not the Holy Spirit; the Holy Spirit is not the Father; but the Father is God, the Son is God, the Holy Spirit is God. That's what Triune is.

See if you can figure out another diagram that shows how that might all fit.

TRUST   *Psalm 22:4*

A great word. *Trust*. Drop the *s* and add an *h*. Trust then becomes truth, another great word.

There's a clear connection between trust and truth. If you're going to trust something, it has to be truth. Trust means to lean upon. When you trust, you lean upon something. If what you lean upon is not "truthful," you are in trouble. Let me explain.

If you decide to get on a swing and pump it real high—I mean r-e-e-e-al high—you better trust the rope or the chain. It better be a "true" rope. Or, it better be a "true" chain. If it's not, the swing will break and you'll come crashing down. You better never trust an untruthful rope or chain!

Or, if you build a treehouse and nail up ladder steps so that you can climb on them, you better be able to trust the steps, and the tree, and the nails, that they are true. True steps. True nails. True tree. If any of those fail you'll come flying down so fast you'll wish you were a bird. But if you trust the truth of the nail, and the steps, and the tree, you can bounce and jump up that tree without fear or hesitation.

Or, if you trust that the doctor is telling the truth when he says the shot will pinch a little but not really hurt, you'll relax. If you don't trust him—if you don't believe he's telling the truth—you'll tense up. Ouch! You will be right and he'll be wrong. The shot will hurt. Or you'll feel like it's going to hurt, and that's almost as bad.

When you trust something, you believe it is the truth and lean on it. You will swing in the swing, jump on the ladder, relax in the doctor's office. You have confidence in the truth. You will trust.

The Bible urges us to trust God (Proverbs 3:5). It says that our spiritual ancestors did. Can you recall a story from Christian history about somebody who "leaned upon God"? I mean that trusted in Him? Think.

What about you? Can you tell a story about yourself that shows you trusted God? If telling one out loud makes you nervous, talk to yourself. Tell yourself about a time you trusted, and you can be sure God will hear, too.

UNION/UNITE/UNITY   *Ephesians 4:13*

How many words can you think of that begin with the letters *uni*? How about the Uni _ _ _ States? Or how about the Plumbers *Union*? *Unite*? A military *unit*? Have you ever heard of people who sing in *unison*? Or people who wear a *uni*form? What about a *uni*corn?

What do you think *uni* means? Let me tell you. It obviously means one.

The unicorn has _____ horn. Uniform means that everyone dresses _____ way. Unison means that the whole choir is singing _____ note or _____ melody. A unit is _____ piece of something. Union means two are made _____ (as in the marriage union). Or a labor union is one in which everyone promises to act together as _____ . The United States is "_____ nation under God."

Now think. What does *union* mean? It means one. That's right.

Almost all words that begin with *uni* have something to do with the idea of one. We believe that the Father and the Son and the Holy Spirit are one, so we call them Tri*une*. They are of one will and one spirit and are, in fact, one God.

God wants us to be *united* with Him. And He wants us to be in *union* with others. That's what Jesus prayed for in John 17:22.

Those three *uni* words are great: unity, union, unite. They explain God's intent toward us and outline the way we should act toward one another. Those words urge one, big, happy family and one life in the Spirit. As a matter of fact, St. Paul got so excited about those three words that, in Ephesians 4:4-6, he lists seven things that are one. Look at that list. Pick out those seven things. Write them down. Applied to our lives, those seven things make us all ____ , too!

VESPERS

Psalm 141:2

Remember matins—that special worship service that takes place in the morning? Years ago, in the monasteries, that service was very early in the morning. Now it usually takes place sometime around six o'clock or even later. It's supposed to be the first worship each day. Could we be getting lazy?

Now, what about vespers? Let's see how good you are at guessing. Which of the following is true about vespers?

1. T F Vespers is a worship service.
2. T F Vespers takes place in the evening after five o'clock.
3. T F Vespers are used today.

The first two statements are absolutely true. The last may not be true in your congregation, but it certainly is in many other places in the world.

Vespers began with the monks and the monasteries of the early Christians. Remember that monk and monastery means "I want to be ____." (See "Matins" if you can't get that word.) Those early Christians had regular worship times. Their early evening worship, the one at about sunset, was called vespers.

Just as matins begin with the same Scripture verses everywhere, so do vespers. The vespers verse is from Psalm 141:2. That verse accents p _ _ _ _ _ and lifting h _ _ _ _ .

Try doing those things. What is the direction your fingers are pointing? Up? Aren't the tips of your prayer-and-lifting fingers pointing up? That's important. Vespers, matins, or any other service of worship always call us to look up.

While God is everywhere (He is omnipresent), a common signal that praying is taking place is looking up. When praying is shown on TV or in movies, the actors are usually looking up. Even though there are no words spoken, you know people are praying because they're looking up. Vespers are a Christian's way to end the day "looking up." Just like matins are a fine way to start the day with a song (it begins, "O Lord, open Thou my lips . . ."), so vespers are a fine way to end with prayers lifted toward the Lord. Start the day with a song. End it with a prayer. You'll find that everything in between is exciting, and that God's blessings will follow you everywhere.

Matins. Vespers. Two great gifts from those ancient Christians who wanted to be alone. They really wanted to be alone with their God.

VESTMENTS   *Exodus 28:2–4*

The 28th chapter of Exodus is almost entirely a description of clothes that the high priests of Israel were to wear. Such clothes! Every thing was special and very costly. I'm not really sure what an ephod (EE-fod) or a breastplate was. I'm not all that clear as to what they looked like. I've seen pictures, but pictures don't always help. Pictures are what someone else guessed they looked like. But when I read the list of materials used to make an ephod, and a breastplate, I know they must have been something beautiful—and costly.

Dig around in Exodus 28, and notice the costly things mentioned. Count all those clothes worn by the priests. All, together, are what we call *vestments*. Vestments is a collective term like "baseball equipment." The term baseball equipment includes, bats, balls, bases, mitts, masks, and other things. *Vestments* includes all the things that high priests wore long ago and all the things their helpers wore as well.

Vestments is still a good word for today. Today, it refers to all the things pastors wear in worship. It includes not only their robes, the stoles, and the other things they wear, but anything their helpers wear, too.

How many different things have we listed in this book so far that would be counted as vestments? We've talked about an alb, cassock, surplice, stole, crucifix. Pastors wear a cross, or medals. Some pastors wear a beautiful poncholike garment called a chasuble (CHAZ-zuh-bull). Of course, there are many who wear a nice suit. That's their vestment. It's usually their best suit. Some even call the garment they wear to worship their Sunday-go-to-meeting clothes. We call them vestments.

I like the word *vestments*. It reminds me of the special things I want to set aside while celebrating the special blessings of our super-special God. He doesn't need me to dress up for Him. The angels could put on a clothing show better than any style show of this world. But we need to have ways of expressing God's specialness to us. Vestments give me that chance.

Is there something special that you wear mostly just for church? That's your vestment. Do your vestments tell how special God is to you?

WAFER (WAY-fur)　　　　　　　　　　　　*Exodus 12:15–20*

Wafer. Wine. Water. Word. Four great words. All begin with *w*. All are used by the Holy Spirit as ways of bringing us faith.

Which of these four words do you recognize? I'm sure you recognize the Word. The Gospel-Word comes to us in Christian witness, in teaching and through the Scripture, and in Christian conversation and helpful advice. The Holy Spirit works in our hearts through all those "words."

The Word and water are B _ _ _ _ _ _ . (Did you write in Baptism?) The Holy Spirit works through water and Word in washing us clean and making us His.

I'm sure you understand wine. The wine, the Word, and the wafer are in the Lord's S _ _ _ _ _ . (Did you write Supper? If you did, that's correct.)

The three *w* words most people are familiar with are Word and wine and water. But the word *wafer* is a little different.

A wafer is a thin, crisp, circle-shaped cake, cracker, or piece of candy. There are candy wafers. There are cookie wafers. But the wafer we're thinking about is a very special wafer Christians love to eat. They eat it when they celebrate the Lord's Supper.

The wafer in the Lord's Supper can be either white or light tan, depending on the flour used to make it. It is almost always shaped in a circle. It is baked from unleavened bread dough. That means there is no yeast.

Many times the wafer has a cross or other design marked on it, reminding us of the death of Christ. That's one of the things that makes the Communion wafer so special. One of these wafers is given to every communicant who kneels at the chancel ready to receive the Sacrament of the Altar.

Have you ever seen a Communion wafer? Ask your pastor, or someone who serves around the altar, to show you one. They might even let you touch one or taste it. That's okay. Until the wafer is specially blessed, it's like any cracker. Anyone can eat it.

Do you recall where unleavened bread shows up in the Bible? There is an exciting story in Exodus 12. In that story, unleavened bread was specially made and eaten the night Israel left Egypt. That special event was remembered as the Passover feast. The night before Jesus died, He remembered the Passover in an upper room with His disciples. He took that unleavened bread and made it something special. He touched it, blessed it, and said, "This is My body." He then took wine and said, "This is My blood." That's how the Lord's Supper was started.

The wafer in the Lord's Supper reminds us of a lot of things: Jesus, the Israelites of old, all the people of God. When we eat that wafer of promise, we are united with all the people of promise and with all the other great promises of God. In a wonderful and miraculous way, the wafer brings us the promised person of Christ. He actually is there. In the wafer. Really. That must be some wafer!

It is.

WITNESS   *Acts 1:8*

A witness is someone who tells what he or she saw happen. If you tell what other people have seen, you are not a witness. You may be a reporter, or a historian, or an announcer; but you are not a witness.

The word *witness* is very easy to understand if you realize that witness has two *I*'s. One *I* is the pronoun *I*. *I* means me. Personally. An I-witness is someone who was there, involved. To be a witness in court, or to other people, you must have personally participated in what you're telling.

The second *I* is spelled e-y-e, like the eye with which you see. An eye-witness has seen something. People are not allowed to give testimony in court about anything they did not actually see. That kind of testimony is called hearsay. Divide that word in two. Someone who is expressing hearsay is telling what they have *heard* other people *say*. You are not allowed to testify, as a witness, if all you can express is hearsay.

Jesus called all of us to be I/eye-witnesses. I am an I/eye-witness when I tell what has happened in my life. That doesn't mean that other things I might report are wrong or are lies. It just means that they aren't the words of a witness.

Let me list some things which might have happened. Place a *W* in front of those examples that are actually witnessing.

_____ 1. George saw an accident and told the policeman who was investigating what he saw.

_____ 2. Two children asked Terry about the Christmas story, and he told them of the birth of Christ.

_____ 3. When asked whether he was a Christian, Warren said yes and told both what he believed and why.

_____ 4. David likes to tell the story of what happened when he was baptized as a baby.

_____ 5. Judy encourages her neighbors to read the Bible and tells them of the joy and satisfaction she receives when she reads it.

I put a *W* in front of the first, third, and fifth statements. Did you? I couldn't do the same for the others. they weren't statements of an I/eye-witness.

Witnessing is so important to the Christian faith that Christians took the Greek word for witness and planted it into their faith language. The Greek word for witness is *marturion.* It sounds like the word *martyr* (MAR-teer). You know what a martyr is, don't you? A martyr is someone who gives his life for what he believes. But more than that. In the giving of their life, they must make a witness to the faith that they have in Jesus Christ. That's what a martyr is.

Have you ever been impressed by the witness of someone else? Tell about it.

WORD OF GOD   *1 Peter 1:24—25*

You would think that something as simple looking as the three words, *Word of God,* would be easy to explain, wouldn't you? Word of God simple means word of God.

Most people think of the Word of God as what He wants us to know and has shared with us through the Bible, or Scripture. They call the Bible, "the Word of God." They are correct. The Bible *is* the words of God. Even though some of the words in the Bible were not spoken by God, we still believe that they are His. St. Paul says that in 2 Timothy 3:16. He says that God inspired the thoughts of the holy writers. Inspire means *breathe in.* God breathed the specific thoughts into the writers of Scripture and led them to state His message correctly.

But the term *Word of God* can also mean something other than the Bible. It can refer to that powerful force by which the world was called into being. Remember how the worlds were made? Hebrews 11:3 puts it this way: "By faith we understand that the world was created by the _____ ."

Our three words may refer not only to the Bible, but also refer to the powerful force by which God created everything that exists.

And there is more. One of the special names by which Jesus is known is "the Word." St. John calls Him that in the first chapter of his gospel. The title *Word of God* is another term used to describe the Lord. It joins the long list of names like Immanuel (God-with-us) and Jesus (Savior) and Christ/Messiah (the Anointed One). There are more. Many more. But right there at the top of the list is the Word of God.

So the term *Word of God* is not simple stuff. How could it be? Though the words are simple and easy to understand, when they are linked together, they can mean any one of three powerful things: Scripture, the creative power of God, Jesus Christ.

WORKS   *Ephesians 2:10*

Charlie knew the rule. His mother had spelled it out very carefully. "You are not to play at Robby's without telling me first." How could anything possibly be made more clear? Yet, one day, Charlie ended up at Robby's and never told his mother

Charlie usually got caught when he did things wrong. This time was no different. Dad was coming home from work that evening and saw Charlie at Robby's. He assumed it was all right. When Dad got home and discovered Charlie's mother was looking for him, he told her where he was.

Can you guess the rest? His mother called Robby's mom. Robby's mom sent Charlie home. Charlie tried to explain why he didn't tell her he was going to Robby's. He said he didn't think he had to ask every time.

"You don't understand, Charlie," said his mom. "Robby is a fine friend. I hope you play with him often. But you can't go there without asking me first. When you do, I don't know where you are. Don't you understand that?" I don't know how he could have misunderstood. But Charlie did.

A lot of times, we are like Charlie, and confuse the clear messages God gives us. Like the clear message God sends us about good works.

God wants us to do good works. He wants us to do good works *because we are saved*, not *in order to be saved*. That message is so clear in Scripture. God wants us to do good works because we are saved.

Confusion on good works is nothing new. When Martin Luther was alive, there were people who were so busy doing good works that they forgot about the good news of salvation in Jesus Christ. Some even thought they could be saved by their good works, without the Jesus-saving work. Luther and others tried to show that we are saved by grace, through faith in Jesus Christ, alone. No work of ours saves.

Well, not long after that argument, there were people who

said you don't have to do good things at all. They said God saves us, and He doesn't care if we do good works or not. Once again, they confused a very clear message of God. God *does* save us. But He also wants us to do good works. He wants us to do things which bless others, show obedience to Him, and help His people live lives that will bring them inner peace.

We must do good works. But we do not do good works in order to obtain the favor of God. We do good works because we have already gotten the saving favor of God. Now, let's see if we can show that.

Do you think you could find a picture of a train in a magazine? A newspaper? Maybe in a catalog? Clip it out. Paste it on a piece of paper. Write the word FAITH on the engine. Write the words GOOD WORKS on the last car. The last car follows the engine. If it's connected to the engine, it goes wherever the engine goes. But it always follows the engine.

Good works follow faith. They *always* follow. It's as simple as that.

Are works important? They sure are. God gave us life in order that we might do them. Isn't that what Ephesians 2:10 says?

WORSHIP *Matthew 4:10*

All that Satan asked Jesus to do was fall down and worship him. If Jesus would worship Satan, He would receive the whole world. All the money. All the gold and jewels. All the toys, food, parks, and swimming pools. Everything. Just for worshiping Satan.

If you can get all that for worshiping, worshiping must be powerful stuff! It is.

One way of understanding worship is by looking at that word itself. Take the first three letters: *wor*. Now add the letters *th* to them. Add those letters here: wor __ __ . What new word do you get? Worth? Worship means to give worth to something. If you worship your bike or your friends or your school, you are giving worth and honor to them. And if you worship God, you are doing the same thing for Him.

Worship can't be shared around. You can't worship a lot of things. Worship has to be aimed at only one thing. That's what Jesus said to Satan. He said, "You shall worship the Lord your God and Him only shall you serve" (Matthew 4:10). There can be only one first place. One winner. One God.

But there's something more about the word *worship* that fascinates me. Take those same first three letters and add a *k*. Do that here: wor __ .

Worship is work. It requires effort. You can't be casual about worship. You must concentrate. Worship requires energy. You have to work at worship: sing with vigorous joy, pray with constant sincerity, listen with hungry eagerness. Worship is work.

There is a lot of difference between just-going-to-church and worshiping our God. One calls for worth and work. Only one. Do you know which?

X/XIAN/XMAS

There are no *X* words in the Bible. Not really. Yet there are. Have you ever seen a sign advertising Xmas cards? Those words mean Christmas cards.

I used to think that anyone who would replace the word *Christ* with the letter *X* was just doing something awful. But I could have been wrong. I'm certainly wrong if people who write Xmas know what they're doing.

The Greek word for Christ looks like this: *xpistos*. That first letter is not an *x*. It is called a *chi*. It is pronounced like the first two letters in Christian. The *p* which is the second letter is not a *p*. It is a Greek *r*. It is pronounced *rho*. Early Christians would often take the first two letters of Christ (the *chi* and the *rho*) and let them stand for Him.

If you know what you are doing, you can get away with talking about Xmas cards. And that special *X* could keep popping up everywhere. You could write words like *Xian* (which would mean Christian) or *X* (which would mean Christ), if you know what you are doing.

I don't get upset when Christians who know use the shortcuts of Xmas, Xian, and X. I warn them that others may not know and understand their spelling. When someone writes Xmas or Xian, or X without knowing, I tell them the real meaning of the word.

Oh, yes, there's another meaning for *X*. At the end of the letters to people you love, there often appear those X's. They stand for kisses. Do you know where they came from?

In the Middle Ages, all legal documents were completed with the mark of St. Andrew, an *X*. That *X* is the shape of the cross on which St. Andrew died. St. Andrew was known for being a good friend to others. He brought his brother to Jesus. During the Middle Ages, each party would put an *X* at the end of a legal agreement and kiss it, as proof that they would keep their word.

In time, people forgot about the legal documents—and about St. Andrew. But they kept the *X* and the kiss. I wonder if the *X* in *Xian* and *Xmas* and *X* could possibly stand for love and kisses from God. Just think. In Christ, God kisses us. *X* marks the spot.

YAHWEH   *Isaiah 12:2*

This is going to be tough to explain. I mean it will really get complicated. We're going to have to try to tie together Yahweh and Jehovah. Let's try.

Jehovah is a word for God that appears in many older Bibles. It means, "the Existing One," or something close to that. In the story of Moses, God was asked what His name was. He said, "My name is *I am*." That means that God exists and has always existed and will always exist. So He is called Jehovah: "the Existing One."

Now comes the hard part. People very long ago were so concerned about taking God's name in vain that, whenever they came to the letters that stood for God, they would not pronounce them. They would pronounce other words. Sometimes, they would say the word *Lord*. They figured that if they never said the word for God, they'd never have to worry about using it improperly. That doesn't make a lot of sense to me, but that's the way they thought.

Now things get a little tougher. When people finally wanted to pronounce the name of God like the Hebrews did, no one knew how to. So they took the initials that looked like Jehovah, added the vowels from the word *Lord*, and wove them together.

Let me show you what happened. The Hebrew word for Jehovah looked like this in writing: *Jhwh*. (There are no vowels in Hebrew writing.) That's where they took the letters from the Hebrew word for Lord, slipped them in between those initials, and came out with the word *Jehovah*.

One more little twist. Modern scholars have decided the name was probably not pronounced Jehovah, but more like Yahweh. In some Bibles, you will find the word *Jehovah*, and in some the word *Lord*, and in some the word *Yahweh*. It all refers to the God who always was, and is, and will be.

I like the name Jehovah or Yahweh. I like thinking about our God as the One who always was. But I best like thinking about the God who always will be. He'll always be there for me. He'll be there with me.

Z.

ZION
Joel 3:17

Most of the time, it's spelled with a *Z*. Zion. Sometimes, with an *S* as in Sion. By either spelling, it appears 156 times in the Bible. Zion/Sion means hill. Not just any hill. It means a special hill in Jerusalem.

The special hill that Zion refers to is the hill in Jerusalem where the temple was built and where King David's palace stood. Everyone, long ago, knew what Zion meant. If I told you I went to the White House, you wouldn't think for a minute I was talking about some building two blocks from church. You would know. Everyone in Bible times knew about Zion.

Sometimes, they would say, "We look for help from Zion." Other times, they would say, "Let us go up to Zion." The first meant they were looking for deliverance from Jehovah, who was in the temple, and who had set King David on the throne on Mt. Zion in Jerusalem. the second meant they were going to the temple. The word *Zion* made people think of their history, of God's promises, and of the great things that He did. It made them think of the fun they had when they worshiped Him.

We have words like Zion, too. I wonder how many places you can think of that make us recall something about our nation or its history. Let me list some words. Behind the words, write a sentence that tells what those words mean. Take a look at them and see if you can come up with some:

1. Plymouth Rock: ————————————————————
2. Valley Forge: ————————————————————
3. Liberty Bell: ————————————————————
4. The Alamo: ————————————————————
5. Pearl Harbor: ————————————————————

I could have listed a lot more. Did you get those? Do you have others to suggest? There are many names that can make us think of deliverance, or victory, or defeat, or national triumph, or safety, or hope, or joy, or knowledge. How about the North Pole? The Wild West? The Great Plains?

Zion meant God, and help, and all the history of His care for His people. It meant that years ago. It means the same thing today. Zion brings to mind centuries of God's care, His plan of salvation in Jesus Christ, His watchfulness over us. Zion is a special place. Zion is a special word. It reminds us of a special God.

Here we are at *Z*; *Z* for the special God. We started out at *A* with absolve. What greater thing does the special God do but absolve us of our sins? From A to Z, He is a great God.